D1636622

AMONG THE CLOUDS

ALSO BY ERIC PINDER

Sheep Football and Other Strange Tales
North to Katahdin
Tying Down the Wind
Life at the Top

AMONG THE CLOUDS

Work, Wit & Wild Weather at the Mount Washington Observatory

ERIC PINDER

Alpine Books
Berlin, New Hampshire

Copyright © 2008 by Eric Pinder

All rights reserved. Except for brief quotations in critical articles or reviews, no part of this book may be used or reproduced in any manner without written permission.

Front cover photographs courtesy of Mount Washington Observatory
Back cover photograph courtesy of Anna Porter Johnston
Additional photo credits on page 99

Library of Congress Control Number: 2008903653

Chapter Two first appeared in *Slate*. Part of this book, in abridged form, first appeared in *Portland*, *Weatherwise*, and *Windswept*.

ISBN 978-0-6152-0459-8

www.ericpinder.com

To Sarah Long
and the summit crew of 1995-2002

Sawdust from the Log
September 21, 2001

7:15 A.M. More snow! Wet, slippery snow and freezing fog have transformed the top of the Rockpile into a winter wonderland overnight, and we can only watch and hope it continues for those of us who can't wait for winter up here. The local fox must be excited too. I can see its footprints running underneath the Weather Room window!

10:15 A.M. Foxes are not all! A large graceful owl escorted me out to the precipitation can this morning! This is a first for me on the summit. Snow has just become freezing rain; it will be a wet and slick day. Perhaps it will put a nice shine on the snowman that the summit crew built in front of the summit cam this morning.

CONTENTS

Sawdust from the Log
September 21, 2001

9:00 P.M. Our friend the owl has stayed with us all day. She was still perched just outside the Tip Top House when I went out to get the precipitation can this evening. Many emails regarding our snowman! We took one person's advice and named him Crag, although there were suggestions to name him List since he was listing dangerously to one side as the temperature rose. Unfortunately he has left us but he'll be back when the next snow flies!

Foreword

HAVE YOU EVER MARVELED at the sky and wanted to know more? I have. Ever since a tornado cut a path through my childhood, I have been fascinated by our atmosphere at work.

My curiosity led to a professional life in the field of meteorology. As a television forecaster, I often get to make the tough call between rain versus snow, among other tricky weather challenges. The city of Boston stands at a crossroads in the sky— the only major metropolitan area subjected to every weather extreme from nasty nor'easters to hurricanes, ice storms, and severe weather. For that reason, local residents tend to be weather savvy, if not weather weary, and have high expectations when it comes to local forecasts. That makes weather prediction in New England especially challenging and exciting work. Besides pouring over data in our weather center and presenting my forecast in front of glaring lights, an impersonal piece of plastic (the camera), and hundreds of thousands of people, I also get to experience weather extremes in the field, producing stories that take viewers beyond the forecast. I have chased tornadoes with researchers in Oklahoma, I have journeyed to the top of Mount Washington (a life Eric knows well!), and I have flown into Hurricane Isabel, to name just a few memorable adventures. I would say that I am hooked! Work never seems like a job—it is my passion.

The same can be said for Eric Pinder. All his life, Eric has been watching the sky with the eye of an intrepid observer and the skill of an adept teacher. He even immersed himself in an extreme climate, working as an observer on Mount Washington. (I only stayed for one night—I can't imagine living on that rockpile!!)

Among the Clouds takes the reader on a charming journey into our atmosphere through the narrative of Eric's adventures in the White Mountains. His tales unknowingly coax the reader into learning about the complexities of weather using a clever wit and a fresh take on our world. No mathematical equations required! Let the winds of discovery sweep you away as you turn the page— Eric conjures up an "atmosphere" for learning. Jump in!

Mish Michaels, CBS4 Meteorologist
Boston, Massachusetts

AMONG THE CLOUDS

Introduction

"DON'T KNOCK THE WEATHER," says comedian Kin Hubbard. "Nine-tenths of the people couldn't start a conversation if it didn't change once in a while."

Fortunately, our weather changes so often and so suddenly, there's always something to talk about.

"One of the brightest gems in the New England weather is the dazzling uncertainty of it," said the curmudgeonly Samuel Clemens, better known as Mark Twain, back in 1876. "You fix up for the drought; you leave your umbrella in the house and sally out, and two to one you get drowned." In the same speech he remarked, "I could speak volumes about the inhuman perversity of the New England weather, but I will give but a single specimen. I like to hear rain on a tin roof. So I covered part of my roof with tin, with an eye to that luxury. Well, sir, do you think it ever rains on that tin? No, sir, skips it every time."

Talking about the weather can be more than mere idle conversation. Weather determines what we wear, where we vacation (Florida is a popular destination for snowbound Northeasterners) and whether we or not we can enjoy an outdoor picnic or hike on a Saturday afternoon. It affects our moods, our economy, and even our politics. Whether the topic is global

3

warming, ice storms, hurricanes, the rising price of heating oil during hard New England winters, or the effect of snow on school closings and football games, we discuss it everywhere from the family dinner table to the local sports bar to budget meetings in Congress.

Weather brings us nature at its best, and sometimes at its worst. "Nature has no mercy at all," says American poet Maya Angelou. "Nature says, I'm going to snow. If you have on a bikini and no snowshoes, that's tough. I am going to snow anyway." And Angelou is right.

Bob Dylan once sang, "You don't need a weatherman to know which way the wind blows," and he was right, too.

You can't control nature, but you don't need to be a professional meteorologist to observe the changing conditions of the atmosphere and to prepare for tomorrow's weather today. With a basic knowledge of the sky, it's possible to look out your window and determine what the next day's weather may bring. The more you know, the more you observe, the more accurate you'll be.

I first learned to read the sky in 1995 when I started a job that put me smack in the midst of stinging raindrops, swirling blizzards, hailstones hurled by hurricane-force winds, and fog almost thick enough to swim in. For years I studied and recorded the weather—and, yes, talked about it, too—at a mountaintop weather observatory in New Hampshire. You could say my career prospects were "looking up."

New Hampshire's Mount Washington Observatory is one of the last human-run weather outposts in this age of computers and automated sensors. My experiences there inspired this book.

Eric Pinder
Berlin, New Hampshire

Snow and rime decorate the Mount Washington Observatory tower. Weather observers must climb up to the highest point, often in hurricane-force winds, to de-ice the instruments.

Looking Up

YOU MAY BE WONDERING: WHY is there an observatory on Mount Washington, of all places? How did I end up living there? Good questions. My parents say they took me to the top of Mount Washington on the Cog Railway when I was three, but I have no memories of that early visit to what later would become my place of employment, my home, and the setting for this book.

I wasn't always interested in weather. Even as a child, though, I had a habit of looking up. In 1980, I was ten years old and lost in space. I wanted to be an astronomer. Or, better yet, an astronaut. Carl Sagan's *Cosmos* series on PBS captivated me; unfortunately, a few years later, college-level calculus did not. I could do the math but couldn't *feel* it intuitively, and for a successful career in astronomy that's not good enough. My soaring hopes of traveling the universe landed with a thud.

Still, I kept looking at the sky. Even with the cheap, four-inch telescope I'd bought as a teenager it was possible to gaze across trillions of miles and millions of years back in time. The rings of Saturn showed up as a tiny, glimmering disk, reflecting light that took hours to cross the solar system and arrive on Earth. It chilled and thrilled me even more to realize that light from the Andromeda galaxy had just ended a two-million-year journey by

6

bouncing off my telescope's mirror into my eye.

One thing I noticed right away was that stars shimmered, while the planets shone with a steady, unbroken light. Why?

The answer, I learned, had more to do with Earth's own atmosphere than with interstellar space. The starlight we see on a clear night passes through turbulent sections of the sky that have different temperatures and densities, and at each boundary the light refracts or "bends." As a result, the stars flicker.

All stars (save the Sun) are so far away that they look like mere pinpoints, much like solitary pixels on a black computer screen. But a planet is close enough to appear as a disk, composed of multiple pixels. Each individual "pixel" on that disk is refracted and bent as it passes through our atmosphere, but the disturbances more or less cancel each other out. Therefore the planet's light shines steadily. Planets don't flicker because they're closer, and therefore look wider, than the point-like flames of the stars.

Some nights, of course, no stars are visible at all. Clouds—or, as frustrated stargazers call them, "that stuff"—block the view. So one day I decided to focus my attention on "that stuff," and discovered it was just as interesting and intriguing as the stars.

Today, I like to think of meteorology as "local" astronomy. Looking at clouds on Earth isn't so different from observing dust devils on Mars or the swirling, red-hued clouds and storms of Jupiter. The only distinction is that the planet we're studying is also the planet we happen to live on.

My interest in both weather and astronomy stayed with me through college and beyond, but it was weather that became my career. Astronomy, though, was my passion.

For years I've worked at the meteorological observatory on the summit of Mount Washington. The alpine weather's fascinating, but the mountain also provides a terrific platform for watching the stars, planets, and the Milky Way—when the summit isn't obscured by fog. With little light pollution and a thinner atmosphere overhead, the stars sparkle. Sometimes observers on the summit can see curtains of white or green from the northern lights, where charged particles pouring out of the nearest star— our sun—collide with our upper atmosphere and ionize it. As one book poetically puts it, the aurora is where "the sun's atmosphere touches our own."

I'm supposed to be watching the weather, but the summit crew and I like to walk onto the observation deck whenever the wind calms and the stars glimmer. Some nights we're even able to watch the path of the space shuttle or the International Space Station overhead. Other nights we see meteors—shooting stars—tiny grains of glowing meteoric rock heated by friction as they enter Earth's atmosphere.

Meteors look pretty, but they don't have anything to do with weather. If you've ever wondered why the study of weather is called "meteorology," while the study of actual meteors is called "astronomy," blame Aristotle. His book *Meteorologica* described everything that fell from the sky, which he called "meteors." Technically, meteors include rain, snow, and hail—not just tumbling pebbles from outer space. (More specifically, rain and snow are considered hydrometeors.)

Aristotle was undoubtedly brilliant, but he was off the mark about a few things. Comets he believed to be atmospheric phenomenon, a strange sort of cirrus cloud high in the sky. He never realized how "high" those comets actually were.

This afternoon on Mount Washington neither comets nor clouds are visible in the sky. As I write these words, high pressure is building into the region, drying up the clouds, promising a fine view of the stars all night. Here on the summit we're enjoying pristine 95-mile visibility with scarcely any wind. Hard to believe that just a few hours ago the wind was gusting to 86 mph and we could hardly see the ends of our noses. Now the sun is setting and the sky is darkening. If all holds to form, the visibility won't be just 95 miles tonight—it will be infinite.

The Peak of My Career
(A Typical Week on Mount Washington)

Monday, June 26

I'VE SPENT MY FIRST NIGHT on the summit this week watching for thunderstorms. The weather map shows a line of showers and electrical storms spanning North America from the southern tip of Ohio down into Georgia, slowly edging east. It's an understatement to say that lightning is hot. At 43,000 degrees Fahrenheit, it heats the cooler air around it so violently that powerful (not to mention noisy) shock waves reverberate across the sky—thunder! Lightning bolts have already struck the southwestern corner of New York State and are soon expected to sizzle across New England.

I'm busy with other chores at the moment—there are measurements to take, data to record and report, memos to write—but I keep one wary eye on the black night sky outside the window. I'm waiting for that first flash—the signal that will prompt me to jump to my feet and run like crazy through the rooms of the observatory, shutting down all the computers. There's one sure way to incur the wrath of our accounting department, and that's to let an expensive research computer get zapped.

When I first started working at the Mount Washington

Observatory in the mid-1990s, we only had a handful of computers and didn't yet have a web page. Now there are no less than 21 computers constantly humming. The last time they were all shut down, the sudden silence amazed me. You don't realize how much background noise all the computers, radios, clocks, and other electrical appliances in your life are making until suddenly they are switched off.

Tonight, the relative quiet in the weather office only magnifies the wailing and shrieking of the wind, just outside the concrete walls. Every hour I put on a coat and go outside to take a weather observation, which is then coded and reported to the National Weather Service. There's something ominous about stepping alone into a wet, black fog, waiting for your eyes to adjust to the dark, watching the beam of your flashlight get extinguished by swirling mist only a few feet away. The wind gusts above 70 mph, tearing at the hood of my jacket and tousling my hair. It roars like Niagara Falls. There's a drenching rain, too, so I might as well be standing under a waterfall. It's unnerving, stepping away from the safety of the tower door and walking across the observation deck. Exposed, unable to see, I can't tell whether or not a massive seven-mile-high monster of a cumulonimbus cloud is looming above me, ready to pounce. Quickly, I collect the data I need and hurry back inside.

I'd forgotten how creepy the night shift can be. Usually I work the day shift. But this weather station is in business 24 hours a day, 365 days a year, and so this week I'm filling in during the overnight hours. That means I must stay awake—and also alert and coherent enough to accurately read instruments and deal with any emergencies—until 4:30 A.M. Not normally a coffee drinker, I might have to raid the kitchen for some caffeine.

A little after midnight, it's time to collect the precipitation can from the middle of the summit cone. Everyone else is asleep.

Even our cat Nin is napping, curled up on an old sweater on the corner of my desk. He blinks occasionally and looks up to see what I'm doing, but clearly has no inclination to accompany me outside. Not while this wind is howling. So I hoist the precipitation can on my shoulder and walk alone down the empty corridor to the front door. Eight hours earlier this section of the building was a noisy hubbub of visitors, park rangers, and hikers. Now it's empty and silent. A light suddenly flickers off to my right, and I stop, startled. But no, it's not the much-anticipated lightning. A TV monitor above the stairs of the summit museum has been left on and is broadcasting static.

As soon as I reach the door and step outside, the fog cuts off the glow of my flashlight at ten feet. The narrow beam, lopped off, resembles a Star Wars lightsaber. That's all I can see. Immediately beyond the edges of that feeble light, there's nothing but shadows. To navigate to the precipitation can, I rely more on my ears than my eyes. The grumbling and sighing of the wind sounds like ocean waves crashing against the shore. To my left, I hear a rhythmic clang clang clang, a noise like the galloping of horse hooves on pavement. I identify it as the cords of a flagpole clanking in the gusts. At least now I know where I am. A moan almost like a human voice joins the cacophony, but it's only a 70-mph gust being funneled between the roof and tower. I stagger out to the precipitation can, buffeted by wind, and then return to the weather room. Nin yawns at me.

Still no sign of lightning. But sometimes it sneaks up on us. The scariest experience I ever had came four years ago. I had climbed to the very top of the tower just after dinner as needles of rain stung my face. My task was to take down a three-cup anemometer, used to measure low-speed winds. We remove it if the wind picks up above 30 mph, to avoid damaging the bearings. The forecast had made no mention of thunderstorms, but suddenly the sky above me lit up like the fourth of July. And there I was, standing in the rain at the absolute highest point in New England on an exposed parapet, holding a wet, metal anemometer. Not exactly the safest place to be. I must have set a speed record for leaping down the ladder and sprinting back inside the tower.

My co-worker, Anna, encountered the same, unexpected, pulse-pounding terror last winter. She was de-icing instruments at the top of the tower, when she saw a "spark" out of the corner of her eye. Her teeth began to hurt, too. That should have been the first clue that what she had seen was no ordinary spark. But it was February, and who expects lightning in February? Her main worry was that perhaps she had accidentally shorted out some electrical wires. So, unaware of any danger, she kept chipping away at the ice. Then the sky exploded once more, and a resonating boom of thunder made it clear that it would be a pretty darn good idea to get back inside.

No staff member has ever been seriously injured at the observatory, but we sure seem to have our share of close calls.

Sawdust from the Log

"It was so blustery that a particularly strong gust actually swept me off my feet and I went about thirty feet before I could stop myself. The temperature has been steadily dropping and is now at a chilly -6 °F. Definitely an exciting night on the Rockpile."

"Around 9:30 there was a sudden, unexpected flash of lightning. Thundersnow—sounds like the title of a James Bond movie. The building is creaking, groaning, and snapping as the temperature drops."

Tuesday, June 27

YESTERDAY, WHILE THUNDERSTORMS WERE rumbling across New England, two hikers got stuck on the summit overnight. Apparently they were so eager to reach the peak that they didn't bother to listen when their brains (and probably their leg muscles) started screaming "Stop!"

People often forget that the pinnacle of a mountain is only the halfway point of any journey, not the final destination. When the wind starts to mutter and growl, and fog suddenly blinds your eyes like a gauze, you're supposed to turn back, not keep climbing to higher elevations where the conditions get even worse. As mountaineer Ed Viesturs once said, "Getting to the summit is optional. Getting down is mandatory."

The two men trapped on the peak last night were running late and probably shouldn't have been hiking in such weather in the first place. They're lucky that Mount Washington actually has shelter at the top. Most mountains don't come equipped with roofs, walls, and softhearted park rangers who grudgingly take pity on bedraggled, windblown hikers. During the night, I forgot they were here in the building; I barged into the storage room where they were sleeping on the floor and accidentally let the door slam behind me. Oops.

Their original plan had been to hike to a nearby Appalachian Mountain Club hut called Lakes of the Clouds. That itinerary changed as soon as the first lightning bolt struck. A 12-million-ton cumulonimbus cloud, billowing up into the stratosphere, blasted the alpine tundra with a brief but dangerous pyrotechnic display. The Lakes of the Clouds are located 1.4 miles down the trail from the peak. That's only a half-hour hike in good weather, but nobody wants to risk a trip across the exposed terrain when lightning is frying the landscape.

To make matters worse, the National Weather Service had just issued a rare tornado watch for Coös County, with a chance of strong winds and one-inch hail. Here at the observatory, our Lexan windows are effectively bulletproof. That protects the glass from shattering when hurricane-force winds hurl golfball-sized hailstones at the windows. But hikers' parkas are *not* bulletproof, and with a forecast like that one, it's best not to be outdoors at all, period. Hiking on mountainous cliffs in foul weather qualifies as sheer recklessness. Anyone can have an unlucky break: a slip, a fall, a sprained ankle. Too often, though, people get themselves into trouble just by ignoring the warning signs in the sky or by being unprepared. Another quote from Ed Viesturs seems appropriate at this point: "Mountains don't kill people, they just sit there."

I'm reminded of the time a different pair of hikers got lost in the Great Gulf Wilderness, at the foot of Mount Washington. They brought no map, no compass, no directions, and no common sense. Instead, they carried a cell phone, a hand-held Global Positioning System unit, and an unjustified confidence in their ability to survive. With all these wonders of modern technology at their disposal, they didn't panic. They called for help. "We're completely lost, we don't know where we are. Well, wait, actually we do know where we are, sort of," and at this point they read off a long string of numbers that sounded like gibberish—it was actually their exact latitude and longitude in degrees, minutes, and seconds—from the display on their GPS unit. "So, um, where is that exactly?"

Without a map, all those numbers meant nothing. It could have been a list of random zip codes for all the good it did them. Had they taken the simple precaution of bringing a map, they could've saved themselves a cell phone fee, a few wasted hours of anxiety and discomfort, and considerable embarrassment. At least they escaped unharmed.

Sawdust from the Log

July 17. "Traffic jam on the Auto Road near six-mile grade, with honking horns and everything. Two cars with jittery drivers going in opposite directions weren't sure they had room to pass each other, so they both just stopped. It's a Saturday; two injured hikers on the mountain (so far)."

THE PEOPLE WHO GET LOST aren't always found in one piece. Reckless behavior and sometimes plain old bad luck can result in sprained ankles, broken bones, hypothermia, and other serious mishaps. These lost or injured hikers often call the observatory for help. To prepare for these accidents and emergencies, the observatory crew needs to take an occasional refresher course in wilderness first aid. That's what's taking place today.

Right now, Anna is practicing her skills at measuring blood pressure. I'm the guinea pig. She thinks she's found an artery in my arm, but there's a problem. She wraps my arm in a sphygmomanometer or "BP cuff," then squeezes until my forearm loses all circulation and nearly falls off. So far that's normal. The problem is that after going through the whole process, she can't hear my pulse. The stethoscope must be in the wrong place. It's only off by a millimeter or two, but that's enough. Unable to detect the pulse point in my arm on a second attempt, Anna starts to get frustrated. Then she gets an idea. "There it is! Don't move," she instructs. Before I can so much as protest "Hey! Wait a minute! What do you think you're d—" Anna has snatched a magic marker off the desk and poked me in the arm. There's now a little black smudge of permanent ink located precisely over the pulse point on my right arm. It'll probably be there for weeks. But the third attempt to determine my blood pressure works perfectly.

The results: 115 over 70.

Bryan, an Emergency Medical Technician from the valley, is up on the summit to instruct us in CPR and other life-saving techniques. In the mountains, we never know when we'll need to use these skills. Case in point: Just a couple days ago a hiker collapsed and died of a heart attack at nearby Franconia Notch. CPR was administered on the spot. Unfortunately, the trailhead (and the nearest road) was over a mile away, and before the rescue team could carry him the full distance over the rocky trail to the waiting ambulance, it was too late. That serves as a reminder that, in the backcountry, not all rescues have happy endings.

Wednesday, June 28

HARRY HUNTER ARRIVED FROM PITTSBURGH and promptly died of exposure on Mount Washington in 1874. He was only the seventh victim of this mountain's savage climate, but his story is unusual because, after his death, his body was not found until six years later.

In 1912, a team of surveyors including John Keenan traveled to the summit. It was Keenan's first day on the job—and, as it turns out, his last. He stepped into a churning fog, less than 100 feet away from safety. His colleagues hollered and yelled, but no answer came. He was never seen again.

We've had weather like that this morning: fog thick enough to swim in. If I reach out my hand, it starts to vanish in the mist. Two of the observatory's interns, Justin and Nate, took a short walk down the trail and could barely keep each other in sight. They were standing right next to each other. "I took a step," Nate tells me, "And when I looked back, suddenly there was no Justin. I could hear his voice coming out of the fog."

What reminds me of the John Keenan tragedy is the fact that a hiker has found some mysterious bones hidden among the boulders behind the Tip-Top building. She gathers them in a bag and carries them to the information desk. The fact that the bones were discovered in close proximity to an old boot raises a few eyebrows. It's reasonable—and a little chilling—to assume that the bones and boot both belonged to the same (deceased) owner. That certainly narrows down the species; you don't see wildlife wearing boots. It's clear that the bones were buried intentionally under the rocks. The implications are grim. More than 100 people have perished on this mountain, mostly due to avalanches, falls, and hypothermia. But we've never heard of anyone being murdered…until now?

As I walk toward the end of the building to investigate, I hear our museum attendant, Laurie, talking on the phone. "We had a hiker drop off some, um, artifacts," she whispers. Three or four customers are browsing the bookshelves in the gift shop, within hearing distance. Until the authorities have learned more, we don't want the gossip to spread. Once the tourists leave, Laurie becomes less cryptic: "It looks like a boot and a hip bone with a socket, and maybe part of a skull, and some other pieces. I don't know what I'm supposed to do with it."

The boot is of Victorian Era vintage: weathered and very old-fashioned. It's certainly not the kind of footwear you can buy at L. L. Bean.

The plot thickens. Speculation changes from A) a hoax, to B) a century-old murder finally come to light, to C) a long-lost hiker from the 1800s, buried by his companions and forgotten, to D) a raven's food cache full of animal bones. The latter option is the least disturbing but fails to explain the presence of the boot. Further excavation uncovers ten more bones, plus a leather strap and strips of old wallpaper. The first batch of bones has already been sent to the valley for analysis. If the artifacts turn out to be human, the state police will drive up to the summit.

Later, of course, it turns out that our cloak-and-dagger guesswork is wrong. Laurie receives a call telling her that the bones belong to…dum da dum dum…an unfortunate ex-moose. The poor animal must have been served for dinner at Tip-Top House sometime in the late 1800s, and its bones and carcass were discarded in a garbage pit. The boot and other relics date from around 1900. We've stumbled upon a long-forgotten Victorian dump…nothing more. So much for an "Unsolved Mysteries" special set on Mount Washington.

It was a weird day even before the bones showed up. Interaction with the public is one of the chief duties of the observatory crew, especially in the summer. It doesn't matter whether the public is finding bones or breaking bones (i.e. their own). In the mountains, you never know who you'll meet, or what crazy things they'll say.

Charlie, a 22-year-old meteorologist, took a walk around the summit earlier in the day. He encountered a middle-aged man and woman sitting at a picnic table. The couple grinned, seeming very friendly and quite pleased with themselves. Charlie soon learned why. They announced, without blushing, that they had climbed the mountain to (I'm phrasing this politely) "join the mile-high club." Actually, the man boasted that they had gazed up at the mountain and whimsically decided that the peak would be a really great place to "boink."

When an unsuspecting park ranger asked the happy couple if they'd enjoyed their visit, probably no tourists have ever answered more sincerely. "It was a pleasure."

A few of the other sightseers were frowning, shivering, wishing they'd packed an extra sweater. But not these two. Certain visitors were unhappy because fog diminished the view. Others arrived thinking they were on Mount Rushmore, and left disappointed after learning they were thousands of miles off course. (Mount Washington is the highest peak in the Presidential Range, so perhaps that's an understandable mistake. Well, no, not really.) And quite a few people have arrived on the summit only to learn that they're terrified of heights. So the mountain experience definitely isn't for everyone. But we now know of at least two vacationers who left the mountain, um, fully satisfied.

Thursday, June 29

YESTERDAY A COLD FRONT PLOWED across New England, smashing against the mountains and chasing storm clouds into the sea. A wedge of cold air brutally shoved aside a warm, moist air mass, clearing a path for sunshine and less humid weather. In the afternoon, a sudden burst of convective energy triggered yet another thunderstorm. Cumulus congestus flattened against the roof of the troposphere, seven miles high. The jet stream—a high-altitude river of wind racing at over 200 mph—sheared off the tops of thunderheads and hurled ice crystal clouds hundreds of miles downwind.

The atmosphere is a violent place. A "front" is the boundary between warm and cold air; it's a word that Norwegian meteorologists borrowed from military terminology after World War I. Air masses fight for territory on the Earth's surface, like armies at war, and that's what reminded scientists in the 1920s of the recently concluded European nightmare.

Six quadrillion tons of nitrogen, oxygen, carbon dioxide, water vapor, and other trace gasses are constantly jostling each other in our sky. Sometimes it feels like the worst of their battles occur right here on Mount Washington. Hence the mountain's nickname, "Home of the World's Worst Weather." Whether or not the mountain really deserves that designation is debatable, but it's true that hurricane-force gusts (74 mph or greater) hammer the peak more than 105 days a year. Yesterday we fell just short of hurricane status, topping out with a gust of 65 at the precise moment that the front rolled into Coos County.

On weather maps, a cold front looks like a long blue curve with jagged triangular spikes stabbing into the east, in the direction the front is moving. The spikes symbolize a sharp spear of cold, wind, and rain. Yesterday's front is now sliding out across the Atlantic, bothering nobody but the fishes (and the fishermen). In its wake, the wind atop Mount Washington shifts to the northwest. Cooler, drier air sweeps down out of Canada. That brings us relief from the oppressive heat of the last week. By "oppressive" I mean temperatures in the 50s, peaking at 63 degrees Fahrenheit on Monday. It rarely gets warmer here. The mountain's all-time hottest mercury reading is only 72 degrees Fahrenheit. In late June, it's usually in the 40s. That's one of the perks of this job: natural air conditioning.

It's hard to believe that only three weeks ago, we were still cranking up the thermostat and shoveling snow. Springtime didn't arrive this year until June 8th. I still remember the day. I was outside taking some measurements and slinging a psychrometer, a device that measures temperature, dew point, and relative humidity. Suddenly—thump!—a block of ice fell off the tower and hit me on the top of my head. An ice storm had struck the mountain the previous night, but as soon as the sun came out, all the ice had started falling off the buildings with loud, brittle crashes. Well, not quite all. In some shadowy corner there must have been one piece left. It broke loose and landed right on my noggin. Just my luck.

I was facing east and never saw it coming. Based on the size of the pieces it broke into after whacking me on the head, I estimate it was about the size of a football. Warm blood started streaming down my forehead into my eyes. I didn't panic. Hurrying back inside, I grabbed some paper towels and held them to my head. The rest of the crew looked at me in pure horror; my face was stained red. However, since I could still repeat numbers and measurements coherently and showed no sign of dropping dead on the spot, they finally determined that it must look worse than it was. Since there was still a weather report to code and file, an intern transcribed the numbers for me while I cleaned myself off and applied pressure to the wound. It's strange to realize how the courses of our lives can be determined by split second actions. Had I walked across that exact spot one second sooner (or later) none of this would have happened—and I wouldn't still be puzzling over the best way to wash bloodstains from Gore-Tex gloves.

The weather has warmed up since that day. In fact, it's warmed up so much—nearly breaking the record high temperatures for several days—that talk at the observatory has turned from winter to global warming. The Earth's average temperature is currently 59 degrees Fahrenheit. But ice core samples reveal that the climate has been both much warmer and much colder in the past. The pendulum swings both ways. Ocean levels fluctuate over time.

We need to remember that heat is energy, and energy, at least in a meteorological sense, is violence. Turning up the global thermostat a notch will give the atmosphere a little extra oomph. Thunderstorms, tornadoes, and hurricanes will pack more of a punch. Everyone's heard the dire predictions of heat waves and rising sea levels. The worst scenarios describe a surging ocean swallowing each tiny Caribbean island like a modern-day Atlantis.

The observatory staff jokes about Mount Washington becoming "beachfront property," thanks to global warming. "Are these mountains below sea level?" we once were asked.

"Not yet!" we replied laughing. Still, there's no doubt that sea level could rise. Any future melting of the polar ice caps, combined with the thermal expansion of water, will mean you'll need to bring snorkeling gear the next time you visit downtown Miami. If the entire Antarctic ice cap melts someday, in our nation's capitol only the tip of the Washington Monument will protrude above the waves. Who knows? If so, Kevin Costner's movie, *Waterworld*, might actually enjoy a revival. But it will be hard to find a theater with dry seats.

FACT TWISTER? The enjoyable movie *Twister* unfortunately got one thing wrong right at the start. In a flashback scene, a worried character shouts, "It's an F5!" He's referring to the Fujita scale, which rates tornadoes; the higher the number, the more dangerous the tornado. There's just one problem. The flashback scene was set in the late 1960s, whereas the Fujita Scale wasn't developed until the early 1970s.

Friday, June 30

A RAPIDLY DWINDLING PATCH OF snow on the northeast slope of Mount Jefferson is pretty much all that's left of winter. I look across the Great Gulf with binoculars and see it sparkling in the sun.

Amazingly, ski tracks still scar the snow's surface. Somebody has trudged five miles up a rocky trail with a pair of skis for the sake of a 20-yard run. It must have been a member of the semi-(in)famous local group of winter sports addicts who challenge themselves to ski in as many consecutive months as possible. Their only rule is that enough snow must exist to allow room for at least 10 turns. So if your skis are bigger than the snow patch itself, you might as well stay home; it doesn't count. The record is 24 months of uninterrupted skiing—that is, if you call a two-second jaunt across pebbly corn snow "skiing."

Patches of corn snow are all that Mother Nature has to offer at the moment. It's been too warm. The last time a "real" winter hit New Hampshire was in 1997, turning this mountain into a skier's paradise (and a summer tour director's nightmare). Old Man Winter dumped 96 inches of snow on the summit in May, effectively canceling the summer season altogether. The boundary of the jet stream—you can usually see this on splashy, colorful weather maps like *USA Today*'s, dividing warmer oranges and reds from cooler greens and blues—dipped far south of the Canadian border. Storm after storm followed the jet stream's path from the Great Lakes into New England, whitening the peaks. Down near the Lakes of the Clouds, the snowy northwest slope of Mount Monroe provided hours of entertainment for the observatory's summer interns. They went sledding every chance they got. One morning I walked into a strangely empty weather office and asked aloud, "Where did everybody go?" Far in the distance, faintly carried on the breeze, I'm convinced I heard an excited chorus of "Wheeeeee!" as our team of minimum-wage college students careered gleefully downhill on plastic sleds.

Humans aren't the only creatures who enjoy frolicking in the snow above timberline. Last winter we witnessed a raven purposefully playing on a snow bank. Ravens are very large and very smart—so smart, apparently, that sometimes they get bored. This one had found a unique way to amuse itself. On top of a small incline just outside the weather room window, the raven tucked in its wings, lay flat on its side, and then *voom!*...down it tumbled and rolled, kicking up a tiny cloud of snow. At the bottom of the hill, the bird then jumped up like an eager child, shook itself off, and waddled back uphill on two stubby legs. It turned around and repeated the maneuver. Over and over. For half an hour. Our interns grabbed their sleds and went outside to join it. (At that point, unfortunately, the raven flew away.)

THERE AREN'T TOO MANY JOBS in this country where it's possible to commute to work by sled or ski. In summer, though, we're forced to hang up our sliding implements and make the trek by truck or on foot. The rigors of alpine transportation are such that it's difficult in the summer (and impossible in the winter) to travel up and down the mountain on a daily basis. As a result, shifts on the summit last eight days straight. I've just finished an unusually long nine-day stint and am ready to go home. I'm out of clean laundry, for one thing, and also out of energy. The observatory workweek can be a tiring one. I doubt I'd find the stamina to sled down today, even if there was snow to sled on.

People always ask what it's like to live on the summit. They want to hear about blizzards, violent thunderstorms, bruised bodies flung across the observation deck by 140-mph winds, reckless skiing escapades, and trucks encased in 10 inches of ice. But I tell them that the appeal of working on a mountaintop isn't so much the extremes. It's the variety. Sometimes the simple, comical sight of a tobogganing raven is reward enough.

Toboggans and skis are all useless today, so four of us head down the mountain in a van. I slump into the front seat, exhausted. Overhead, the ravens are swooping and gliding on warm currents of air. I can still see the observatory's cat, Nin, perched on the radiator in the weather room, his eyes flitting back and forth as he follows the ravens' flight. Poor Nin doesn't realize that they're bigger than he is. The ravens could probably lift him in their talons and carry him away, like the flying monkeys in *The Wizard of Oz*. Nin has trouble enough with smaller game. He's a lap cat, not a hunter. Soon the van rounds a corner, and both the ravens and Nin disappear from view...until next week.

As we travel down the mountain, the climate and scenery

change swiftly. The air is thicker here, and the temperature is higher. Bleak, boulder-strewn tablelands spotted with tiny clumps of leftover snow soon yield to evergreens and finally to lush, leafy hardwood trees. It's like visiting a different planet.

We finally reach the bottom. The van door opens, and the June air rushes in with surprising intensity. I feel like I've just opened an oven door. It's only 80 degrees Fahrenheit but on my skin—acclimated for nine days to temperatures in the 40s and 50s—it feels hot enough to bake a cake. I let out an involuntary "whew!"

One of my coworkers from the valley laughs at me. "This is the warmest air you've felt in a while, huh?"

I suddenly realize I'm still wearing a fleece jacket from the top. Sure won't need that down here. I take it off and fling it into my car. At long last, it's time for a day off. Time to collect a paycheck and rejoin civilization. I can't help wishing, though, that civilization wasn't quite so darn hot.

Avalanches and snowdrifts bury the Mount Washington Auto Road each winter, making the weekly trip to the summit much more challenging. The summit crew's favorite way to commute home from work requires a vehicle with no wheels. Illustration by Jon Lingel.

A Punishing Storm

I'VE ALWAYS BEEN TOLD the safest thing to do if you're caught in a thunderstorm while out in the woods is to squat on the ground away from open spaces, or, if that's not an option, to at least go camping with someone taller than yourself.

That advice didn't help anyone last summer in New England. As severe thunderstorms pounded New Hampshire, the sky sizzled with electricity and wind-blasted tree branches smashed around everywhere.

It was the most dramatic display of wind, rain, and lightning I've ever seen—and I've seen some pretty darn good ones.

Fortunately, I had the good sense to ride out the storm in the shelter of my home! A glance at the radar that evening showed an arc of thunderstorms streaking across the country from the Dakotas to Maine. The National Weather Service called it a mesoscale convective complex and issued a severe thunderstorm warning. But I knew better.

The simple fact is this: Zeus had plans for a fireworks display. Despite my modern education and a working familiarity with meteorology, I was ready to get down on my knees and beg Zeus for mercy. Because, boy, did he sound angry.

Perhaps you don't think I'm serious, but I am.

It all began quietly enough, with hardly a breath of wind. Suddenly, the maple tree danced and swayed like Elvis learning to disco. The area was soon hit by a downdraft, which is a surge of cold air flushed out of the middle of the cloud by falling raindrops. Using the Beaufort scale, I estimated wind speeds of 50 mph. In an instant, I was soaked by rain shooting in through an open window.

Call it the "Rain of Terror," because the precipitation just didn't stop. I tried to look at the bright side. On my to-do list of chores, I mentally crossed off the line "wash car," with a grateful nod in Zeus' direction. Unfortunately, Zeus misinterpreted my little prayer as "wash car away."

He intended to wash everything else away, too, apparently, as streets turned into rivers. I noticed a bright orange traffic cone and numerous tree branches drifting away among the flotsam. Meanwhile, the sky flickered every two to three seconds like a giant neon sign gone bad.

In the parlance of weather observation, there are official types of lightning, and this storm in-clouded—er, included—them all: in-cloud, cloud-to-ground, cloud-to-cloud. I even saw examples of cloud-to-tree, cloud-to-radio-antenna, and cloud-to-neighbor's-house.

Much worse was the dreaded "collateral damage" lightning (technically known as "cloud-to-tree-branch, tree-branch-to-car, car-owner-to-insurance-office, insurance-office-to-raise-rates" lightning).

One fat sugar maple just up the street escaped being zapped, but the wind knocked it over just the same. Inconveniently, it toppled the power lines. Pop! Out went the town's lights. The electricity stayed off for 16 hours, and we were powerless to do anything about it.

But Zeus wasn't finished yet.

The next afternoon, a second batch of thunderstorms materialized. This time, it didn't hit us all at once. Clouds go through several stages of development before attaining the "status" of full-grown thunderstorms. That's why, when these monsters of meteorology finally surge above the lowest layer of atmosphere, the troposphere), we say they've reached the "statussphere."

In unstable air, the familiar popcorn cumulus clouds progress through a very predictable sequence—from *cumulus humilis* ("humiliating flat clouds") to *cumulus congestus* ("clouds about to sneeze") to *cumulonimbus incus* ("thunderstorms"). When the sky is full of these clouds, it's categorized as *cumulus tunumerous* or *cumulus allaroundus*. Before long, you're likely to get (in the words of AccuWeather meteorologist Elliot Abrams) *cumulus rainuponus*.

Of course, the scientific terminology is just one way of making sense of an incredibly intimidating force of nature. When it gets really bad, my instincts tell me to resort to ancient Greek mythology to explain the mechanics of weather. Sure, the NOAA weather radio was full of technical chatter about bow echoes and wind shear. But to most listeners, terms like "mesoscale convective complex" were, well, too complex. As I heard one tourist complain, "It's all Greek to me."

Exactly, I thought, and tipped my hat to Zeus.

Now, if only I could find my car.

Calling the Clouds Names

A pharmacist, chemist, and amateur naturalist named Luke Howard first categorized clouds based on their shape in 1803. He named clouds cumulus ("heap"), stratus ("layered"), cirrus ("wispy," "curly", or "lock of hair"), and nimbus ("precipitation bearing"). With some modifications, we still use basics of his classification system today.

Above: The meteorological symbol for a thunderstorm.

ONE WARM SUMMER NIGHT on Mount Washington, towering cumulus clouds were billowing up all around the summit. We escaped with just a brief shower and a few minutes of pea-sized hail. But then the real excitement started.

Radar showed a few storms passing just south of the mountain, about 30 miles away, but we had starry skies overhead. I went out onto the observation deck and the sky was black, featureless—until lightning in the distance flashed. Each flash illuminated the outline on the horizon of a castle-shaped cloud that must have been six miles tall. The flashes were in-cloud lighting. It was like seeing an x-ray of a cloud. The light show continued for 40 minutes.

The Bald Truth about Ben Franklin

BENJAMIN FRANKLIN WASN'T ALWAYS BALD. But by the time he was important enough to sit for portraits, his head was as shiny as a bowling ball. That's why book covers, illustrations, and TV reenactments almost always depict our eccentric Founding Father as middle-aged and follicle-free.

Franklin's hairline steadily receded as his notoriety grew. The multitalented Franklin soon achieved fame not just as a statesman, but as an inventor, scientist, writer, publisher, and eccentric American genius. In fact, he wore so many different hats, you'd think we'd be seeing less of his forehead.

His first career was as a printer—and wiseacre. Back when he still had hair, Franklin was the Yogi Berra of his day. His quips in the pages of *Poor Richard's Almanack* rarely failed to conjure up a smile.

"Make haste slowly," he joked.

"Many would live by their Wits, but break for want of stock."

"Fish and visitors smell in three days." Well, usually. In September 1752, Franklin noted that fish and visitors would have taken two whole weeks to turn smelly. That was the month when England and the American colonies switched from the Julian calendar to the more accurate Gregorian calendar, shortening the month by eleven days in order to bring the calendar back in line with the seasons. Franklin's neighbors panicked. They feared financial chaos as a result of the "lost" days. But Franklin calmly remarked that the time seemed to fly by. "It is pleasant for an old man to be able to go to bed on September 2, and not have to get up until September 14," he joked.

The Yogi Berra of his day evolved into the Thomas Edison of his day. Franklin once hitched a counter to the wheels of a horse-drawn wagon and in doing so invented the odometer, clicking off the miles over the rutty, muddy roads of the eighteenth century. He dabbled in medicine, correcting his own dimming vision by inventing bifocals. He even invented a urinary catheter to relieve the suffering of his brother, who had kidney stones.

With so many ideas, it was as if a metaphorical light bulb constantly was glowing above his head. Not that he or anyone else in the 1700s would have understood the metaphor. Light bulbs did not yet exist. But they would someday, thanks in large part to Franklin's study of electricity. His experiments helped "spark" an interest in electricity among future scientists, including Edison.

During that same shortened month of September 1752, Franklin installed on his roof one of his most practical inventions: the lightning rod. His real claim to fame had occurred during a related experiment earlier that summer: the famous kite-flying-in-a-thunderstorm moment.

They say lightning never strikes twice (which isn't even true). Franklin was lucky it didn't strike once.

Or perhaps luck had nothing to do with it. A recent Franklin biography by Tom Tucker [*Bolt of Fate: Benjamin Franklin and His Electric Kite Hoax*] claims that the kite story itself, not the lightning rod, may be Franklin's most famous "invention." The experiment, Tucker discovered, cannot be repeated in the exact manner Franklin describes. Tucker speculates that Franklin may have made up the whole tale to mislead a rival.

Shocking, if true. Is Franklin's kite as apocryphal as George Washington's cherry tree?

I have my doubts. But one fact is certain. Flying a kite in a thunderstorm is dangerous, but in Philadelphia in 1752 it was not illegal.

Therefore, Franklin was not charged.

The key to good parenting is spending time with your children. Benjamin Franklin and son fly a kite together...in a thunderstorm.

Feeling the Pressure

THE ANNOUNCEMENT CAME ON the first day of class, when we received our schedules. No one liked it, but there was no choice, no escape. For the rest of the year, all students were required to take a 45-minute nap in the morning, whether we wanted to or not. We were in the tenth grade that year, almost adults, and suddenly our school was treating us like children again. Nap time for high school students? No one had ever heard of such a thing. But at our school, it was a graduation requirement.

We called it "chemistry class."

I'm not sure if it was the subject matter, the drone of the teacher's voice, or just the usual surly drowsiness that teenagers express whenever an adult is speaking. Something about chemistry class always put us to sleep. Our teacher—let's call him Mr. Erg— liked to repeat and repeat the basic points of each lesson, long after we were sure we had them memorized.

One day, after he had gone over the definition of Avogadro's number for, oh, about 6.02×10^{23} times, our eyes began to glaze. Everyone prayed for the lunch bell to ring and release us from our restless slumber.

The bell never rang, though, and I was nodding off and about to embarrass myself by falling out of my chair when an unexpected noise woke me up. Two metal cans clanged together. Mr. Erg was taking them out of a cabinet on the far side of the room. Around me, my classmates started to stir. Something was up.

We focused our eyes on the front desk. The teacher had placed one of the cans—which turned out to be a large gasoline can—on the table. The second, smaller can contained a Bunsen burner.

Soon he was playing with fire—literally. He turned on the Bunsen burner, which shot a strong white flame at the bottom of the metal gasoline can.

The can was empty, of course. Into the can he now poured a thin layer of water. Heated to the boiling point, the water expanded and changed to steam. A plume of white steam rose through the opening at the top, expelling all the air from inside. Something interesting was about to happen.

Mr. Erg was wearing oven mitts on his hands. He quickly capped the can and switched off the burner. The water vapor began to cool. As it cooled, it condensed, contracted, and dripped back to the bottom of the can as a liquid. The gasoline can was now empty, or nearly so. Hardly any air remained inside. Our teacher had created a vacuum.

Air, he explained in his usual repetitious way, was pressing down all around us. It was pressing down around us. All around us the air was pre—well, you get the idea. The standard sea-level air pressure of 14.7 pounds per square inch pushed inward against the can, but there was no longer any internal air pressure pushing back.

Mr. Erg backed away from the table. We waited in suspense. What would happen?

Pop. Crack. The metal walls of the gasoline can imploded. Invisible fists started pummeling the can's surface, punching it first here, then there. To our eyes, it looked like a ghost was playing with it, knocking it back and forth. The can jumped off the table and continued to squirm on the floor. Two minutes later the can was crushed. Nothing had touched it—nothing but the seemingly empty air.

There's more going on in "empty" air than we usually realize. Air is invisible, so it's easy to take it for granted. We walk through it effortlessly, and unless we're trying to read a newspaper outside or fly a kite on a windy day, we rarely notice the quintillions of air molecules constantly flowing around and ricocheting against our bodies. But add enough nitrogen, oxygen, and water vapor molecules together and they finally start to matter.

A sudden change in air pressure can crush a gasoline can in a chemistry classroom—or stir up a hurricane over the warm waters of the Atlantic. A sharp drop in air pressure is often the first thing we notice when the winds begin to howl on Mount Washington.

It was here on the summit of Mount Washington that I recently had a chance to repeat that long-ago chemistry experiment. This time, instead of a gasoline can I used a five-pound plastic jug of Durkee's Marshmallow Fluff. And instead of removing all the air pressure from inside the container, I removed it from the outside.

It was late October, the start of the winter season on Mount Washington, and a food order had just arrived at the observatory. The crew and I were busily putting away a truckload of cereals, sauces, fruits, meats, and other items, which would be the bulk of the winter food supply. We were almost done, just a few more boxes to go. I lifted up a jug of marshmallow fluff, intending to put it on the shelf, then immediately dropped it in disgust. The jug's lid had popped open, and the marshmallow fluff was leaking out and dripping down the sides. A sugary goo was all over my hands.

Yes, it was a sticky situation. One of the summit crew saw my predicament and laughed. "The great thing about fluff is that it's whipped at sea level, and it's full of air bubbles." He pointed to the can, which was bulging outward. "So it expands. It oozes."

Air pressure decreases as elevation increases. The pressure atop Mount Washington is only about 11 pounds per square inch, compared with 14.7 at sea level. That's what had caused the goo to break free—and to get all over my hands when I unwittingly picked it up. I reached for a paper towel.

My hands weren't the only things getting sticky that afternoon; so was the air. Humidity was on the rise. A storm was approaching from the west, and the blue ink of the observatory's barograph took a steep dive as the clouds thickened and fog swirled around the summit. The fluff continued to ooze outward while the pressure dropped.

The arrival of this storm helped me recall yet another lesson from high school chemistry class. Avogadro's law states that equal volumes of all ideal gases contain the same number of molecules at the same temperature and pressure. So if you add a few water vapor molecules—humidity—you must first remove an equal number of nitrogen or oxygen molecules to make room. The result: Humid air is lighter than dry air.

It seems counterintuitive, but it's true. The atomic weight of a water molecule is 18. Nitrogen molecules, which make up nearly 80 percent of our atmosphere, have an atomic weight of 28, and the O_2 we breathe is heaviest of all with an atomic weight of 32. When dank air and storm clouds full of water move in overhead, the weight of the air drops and so does the air pressure.

That's an oversimplification, of course. There's much more at work in the atmosphere. The air is always churning, the temperature always changing. Upper-level divergence and lower-level convergence create a rising suction that accounts for most of the drop in pressure during a storm. Condensation within a rising, billowing cloud also releases heat into the atmosphere, making air expand, giving it more buoyancy. Avogadro's law is really just one small piece of the puzzle.

Still, I'd forgotten so much from high school that it was nice to realize I could still recall one lesson from chemistry class, so many years later. Perhaps all that drilling and memorization came in handy after all. Thanks, Mr. Erg.

TRY THIS EXPERIMENT. If you ever have the opportunity to drive up a mountain like New Hampshire's Mount Washington or Colorado's Pike's Peak, bring along an unopened bag of potato chips. Inside, the air is pushing out with a pressure of about 14.7 pounds per square inch (depending on where it was originally bagged or bought, minus any leakage). By the time you reach the top, the bag should be bulging like a balloon. It may even pop because the inside pressure is now greater than the outside pressure.

That's exactly what happened one winter when I was leading a trip up Mount Washington in a snow tractor. We brought along a bag of potato chips. At the bottom of the mountain, elevation 1500 feet, I told the group, "Keep an eye on the chips. The bag will probably explode before we get to the top."

They thought I was joking. But the potato chip bag started to bulge as we climbed higher. At 4000 feet it looked like a balloon. Someone poked it, but it didn't pop. "I don't think it's going to go," he said. "That plastic looks pretty strong." He sounded disappointed.

At 5000 feet, someone else said, "I'm hungry. Can we eat

them?"

"Only if the bag pops," I replied.

Around us snow was tumbling and wind was swirling. The trip to the summit was taking longer than usual, and after a while we forgot about the potato chips and started talking about other matters. Finally we rose above the clouds, scraped ice off the snow tractor's windows, and could see the observatory only a quarter mile away. We were almost there.

Just as we were climbing up the last slope toward the front door—*bang*! Everyone jumped in his or her seat, startled. It sounded like a gunshot. Then we all laughed.

Apparently, an 18-ounce potato chip bag sealed at sea level will burst at 6,270 feet. Everyone enjoyed the unexpected snack.

A Bombardier snow tractor plows through snowdrifts and avalanches on the Auto Road. The journey to the summit typically takes an hour and a half in perfect weather. Snowdrifts and poor visibility can lengthen the trip by several hours. Good thing we packed some food.

Brain Freeze

FOR YEARS I'VE LIVED and worked on the windswept summit of 6,288-foot Mount Washington, New Hampshire. You could call it the peak of my career, or the coolest job in the world. You could even say that my job is a breeze. (Mount Washington is famous as the site of the world's fastest surface wind.) All I have to say is that I'm having an ice time.

Technically my job is to monitor the weather. But daily duties also include rescuing lost hikers and giving directions to the thousands of tourists who visit the mountain each year.

Tourists are affectionately nicknamed "goofers" by the rangers, guides, and meteorologists on the summit. When a tourist has a question, the weather observatory or the state park rangers' desk are the first places they go. The funniest questions get written down and circulate amid gales of laughter (Force 10) during off-hours.

"Do you ever get moose up here?" one man asks. Yes, sometimes, the ranger on duty answers. The man pauses, then says, "How do you get them up here?"

One foggy day, a hiker staggers up to the summit, wearily drops his pack by the visitor's center door, and asks, "Is this the bottom?"

A second sightseer wonders, "Is the summit on top?"

"This is my first time up Mount Washington. What do I do now?"

"Is the trail to the bottom downhill?"

"Does the wind ever get so strong that you won't let people under a certain weight out of the building?"

"Are the hiking trails manmade?"

A narrow, 7.6-mile road up Mount Washington allows sightseers to reach the peak the easy way, without the sweat and effort of climbing up on foot. Each summer, the road brings a few people completely unfamiliar with the concept of hiking.

"How much does it cost to walk down?"

"Why does the road go so close to the edge?"

"I'm not a hiker. Am I allowed to talk to you?"

"Do hikers walk up?"

"I hiked all the way up the yellow trail. Aren't I entitled to a ride down?"

"I see people outside. How do I get there?"

"Who cut down all the trees up here? Was it for firewood?"

"Where does the air stop?"

Some tourists are literally "lost" causes. A man inquires, "Which of those mountains out there is Everest?"

On a clear day, after a ranger explains to an admiring crowd that the visibility is 130 miles, allowing views of Maine, Vermont, Quebec, New York, and Massachusetts, a woman asks, "Can we see New Hampshire from here?"

"What's the name of this mountain again?"

In ancient times, people climbed mountains to ask the old, wise, long-bearded hermits who lived there for advice. Well, my colleagues and I aren't old, most of us aren't bearded, and I don't know if we're wise. But feel free to ask us questions. Mount Washington is one place you can be sure that the answers, my friend, are indeed blowing in the wind.

Some summer visitors arrive on foot via the Appalachian Trail and other routes. (You can usually identify these visitors by their smell.) Others drive up in a car on the Mount Washington Auto Road. Many others enjoy the view while riding the Cog Railway. As the Cog huffs and puffs up the slopes, weather observers on the summit identify all the cloud-like smoke and steam as "cumulus bituminous."

White Snow, Red Leaves

LARA'S QUESTION TOOK ME completely by surprise. I stammered, my mind racing for an answer. There wasn't much time. She always liked to ask the tough questions, but this one was the toughest yet. Now she was getting impatient. I knew what would happen if I said the wrong thing.

She was about to give up on me when I desperately blurted out, "Bobtail!"

That, of course, was the correct answer. The question: "What is the name of the horse in the song *Jingle Bells*?" We were in college, late one winter evening, playing Trivial Pursuit. Lara tossed the playing cards in the air in disgust; the others in the room laughed, and I grinned in triumph.

Meteorologically speaking, it was the perfect moment for a question about Christmas carols. Outside, away from our game and the warmth of the radiator, it had begun to snow—the first snow of the season. Flurries swirled in the December air, and the puddles along the walkways of Hampshire College hardened into ice.

I can remember very few blizzards during my college years. In the late 1980s and early `90s, while I was winning Trivial Pursuit games and earning a degree, terms like "global warming" and "climate change" were first starting to appear in newspaper headlines. Politicians, scientists, and businesses were beginning to bicker about whether the climate was changing, and if so, how much. It's a quarrel that continues today. Forgive the pun, but sometimes the discussion about global warming gets, well, heated.

Our local winters do seem warmer than they used to. But I wonder. How accurate are memories of long-ago winters? Back in the days when we had to walk to school uphill both ways, blizzards were more severe and more frequent than they are today. Or so most people say, regardless of when they were born. Is it true?

Thomas Jefferson thought so. "Snows are less frequent and less deep," he noted in 1782. "They do not lie, below the mountains, more than one, two, or three days, and very rarely a week. They are remembered to have been formerly frequent, deep, and of long continuance. The elderly inform me the earth used to be covered with snow about three months every year."

Bing Crosby agreed. He sang longingly about wanting a white Christmas "just like the ones we used to know." *Used to*, implying that it wasn't that way "now." This was in 1942.

Our memories may recall snowier winters, but memory is sometimes fickle. Historical weather records are more objective. These records tell us that most places get the same amount of snow "now" as they did "then." On Mount Washington, the snowfall of the new millennium differs little from the snowfall measured by Sal Pagliuca back in 1932-33, the year of the observatory's founding.

Ah, but sometimes statistics don't tell the whole story. As Mark Twain once said, "There are three kinds of lies: lies, damn lies, and statistics." Perhaps our memories aren't completely at fault after all. It's probably true that childhood memories tend to exaggerate the size of snowdrifts and snow banks (we were all a lot smaller then), but it's also true that snowfall statistics alone fail to answer an important question: How long does the snow stay on the ground?

The 1960s and early `70s were famous for killer snowstorms. In the winter of 1968-69, more than 540 inches of snow fell on Mount Washington alone. More importantly, the snow that fell stayed put. Snowfall totals haven't changed much in the past 30 years, but snow cover is a different story.

In "the old days," there were no (or fewer) mid-winter thaws. No brown grass in January, no rivers of melting slush on the Mount Washington Auto Road. Decades ago, I remember it snowing and staying on the ground, turning the landscape of the Northeast into a tundra-like replica of Greenland for months at a time. Next time it snowed, the snow cover got a little deeper. Often the uninterrupted snow cover lasted till spring.

In more recent years, after a snowfall it warms up or rains; next time it snows the snow cover has to start from scratch. So perhaps it looked a lot snowier in winters past, simply because we didn't have many mid-winter thaws or cold rains.

Or maybe the memory does play tricks. Dylan Thomas in *A Child's Christmas in Wales* said it perfectly: "One Christmas was so much like another in those years that I can never remember whether it snowed for six days and six nights when I was twelve or whether it snowed for twelve days and twelve nights when I was six."

I can't remember for certain, either. It's hard enough remembering the name of the horse in *Jingle Bells*.

Snow has arrived early in the North Country this year. I awoke one morning in early October to see a dusting of ice crystals in Gorham. Snow-capped Mount Washington loomed outside my window. I watched the flurries falling against a backdrop of blazing red and yellow leaves. The fall foliage was still at its peak.

Hundreds of red maple leaves and yellow birch leaves swirled in the wind along with a million tumbling snowflakes. White snow, red leaves. Being a fan of winter, I liked it.

EVERYONE IS USED TO different sorts of weather, particularly winter weather. An inch of snow on the road in Plymouth, New Hampshire, would scarcely be noticed. In Columbia, South Carolina, it would paralyze the city.

My friend Sarah was in South Carolina when a blizzard struck. She soon learned that most people in South Carolina were not used to driving in snow. Cars veered off the road at all sorts of angles. Some people were just standing by the roadsides, helpless, staring at the crust of ice obscuring their windows. They wondered what to do about it.

Sarah decided to help. She pulled a convenient, handheld ice scraper out of her glove compartment and in just seconds had cleared off several people's car windows. They all stared at that strange, miraculous object in her hand as if it was some futuristic gadget out of a Star Trek episode. "Where did you get that?" everyone asked.

"I'm from New Hampshire," she replied. There, every gas station and grocery store sells them. No car's glove compartment is complete without one.

Snow Job

A WEATHER OBSERVER'S DAILY routine on Mount Washington includes informing hikers and skiers of the latest avalanche conditions. In winter, checking and updating the latest avalanche conditions becomes second nature.

I was no longer living on the mountaintop when a blizzard struck New Hampshire early one December. But old habits die hard. The storm dumped four feet snow on my town in just twenty-four hours—and that was on top of the nearly three feet of snow deposited by another nor'easter the previous week. Roads vanished under the drifts. The wind howled. It felt like I was on the summit again. Old memories surfaced. I grabbed a shovel, wrapped a scarf around my face, and slipped (literally—but fortunately the deep snow provided a cushion) back into my old routine. So much snow fell that I felt compelled to write and distribute my own avalanche advisory. It said:

Avalanche danger for Berlin, NH, is high today. Natural and human-triggered avalanches are likely. Greatest danger exists underneath porch roofs and near the tops of cars. People shoveling out their cars are advised to use caution...

After the storm, the four cars in my parking area (including mine) were completely buried. Not even the vaguest outline of cars remained. There was just a giant, featureless block of snow about eight feet tall and 30 feet long. Somewhere inside was my car.

Five minutes into the excavation, my shovel finally hit something solid. I saw blue paint.

It took about 40 minutes to dig out. Even when the sides were clear, there was still a three-foot block of snow covering the car's roof. I was looking up at this mound, resting a moment, when a crack appeared and the block of snow started to calve like an iceberg and fall right toward me. I didn't get out of the way in time.

I can just imagine the headline: BERLIN MAN BURIED IN MASON ST AVALANCHE WHILE DIGGING OUT CAR.

I've seen avalanches before, but that's the first time I've been caught in one in the parking lot.

Rime covers a truck on the summit of Mount Washington.

Sawdust from the Log

November 24. "The aurora borealis put on a show tonight that is unrivaled by anything that I have ever seen before. It was first spotted at 2:45 A.M. and extended across about 60 degrees of the northern horizon in colors of green and red. At times the shimmer of it reached halfway down into the southern sky! It was so bright that the stars were not visible behind it and it cast indistinct shadows on the observation deck. Half of the sky was illuminated a brilliant pale green mottled with crimson and it shimmered and danced majestically. This was a night I will never forget."

November 25. (The handwriting changes.) "It was the most spectacular aurora ever seen in New England. Curtains of green and red danced on the horizon, leaping, glowing, and filling half the sky. That's what they told me the next morning. I slept through the whole thing."

The day-shift observer starts work at 4 A.M. A beautiful sunrise above a rippling sea of clouds almost makes up for sleeping through the northern lights.

Out of Joint

TOGETHER WE WERE SCRAMBLING up the steep rocks of the Lion Head trail on a December morning when I realized that I'd made a bad mistake.

The weather wasn't the problem—yet. I was still warm and comfortable in my heavy coat, wool hat, wind pants, and gloves. My companions were content, too. Everything was perfect. The sun was cold but bright, glinting off the ocean 80 miles away and casting long, black shadows behind the hills of New Hampshire and Maine. What a day to climb a mountain!

We stopped for a moment and listened to the wind surge through the evergreens in the basin of Tuckerman Ravine. The whole forest below us was inhaling and exhaling with slow, patient breaths. By contrast, I was breathing hard and fast; my lungs strained with the effort of the climb. Huffing and puffing, I reluctantly turned my eyes away from the snowy landscape behind me and focused on the rocky trail ahead.

That's when the trouble started. I was in a hurry, but my companions were not. I quickened my pace in spite of their protests. The Observatory's summit crew was expecting me by 12:30, and I had to be there. My METAR certification was about to expire. [METAR is a French acronym for "meteorological airways report."] Every 60 days we're required to file a few official weather reports, and I'd promised to take care of the 12:30 synoptic observation. I was running out of time.

My companions didn't care. They started to complain with every step. The only time they were quiet was when we stopped to stretch or rest. The farther and faster I went, the more they protested. I tried to tune them out and listen again to the peaceful sighing of the wind, but they were impossible to ignore. They wouldn't turn back, and I couldn't leave just them behind. I was stuck with them.

I'm talking about my knees. They were my only companions that day.

The damage to my knees first occurred years earlier on a different mountain, when I had made another bad mistake. A growling eight-mile-high cumulonimbus cloud had appeared unexpectedly, filling the sky with lightning and hail. To escape, I had sprinted down the mountain, leaping from boulder to boulder. Each step drilled my legs like a jackhammer. My knees never forgave me.

Since then, my knees have always insisted that I use a walking stick or ski poles on long hikes. That was my mistake this morning. In the rush to get to the summit, I'd forgotten to bring either. All I had was a 35-inch ice ax—a poor substitute for a walking stick on the hard boulders. My knees were paying the price.

To get relief, though, all I had to do was stop and stretch. It could have been much worse. Some people I know experience knee pain whenever the weather changes (and what a horror that would be on windblown Mount Washington). "A big storm's coming," they predict as they clutch their knees in agony.

Fluid, gas, and tissue around our knees and other joints actually expand or contract with changes in air pressure, just like a barometer. Some people are sensitive to the change. A sudden drop in barometric pressure before an approaching storm makes their joints swell, announcing a change in the weather. You could joke that some people receive tomorrow's weather forecast on a "knee to know" basis.

It must be a mixed blessing. My own knees were telling me nothing useful about the weather as I continued to race toward the summit. They merely hurt.

Maybe, I thought with a grimace, it was time for surgery. Weeks earlier, a friend had described her "new knee," after an operation and weeks of recuperative therapy. I had resisted the suggestion. (I'm too young to have knee problems, darn it. All knees should come with a 50-year warranty. If I can find the receipt, I'm going to take this pair back.)

Wincing a little, I advanced toward the summit. The wind began to blow in my face, almost pushing me back down the trail. Uncountable numbers of air molecules filled every sudden gust. The clouds thickened. Somehow I limped all the way up to the observatory and finished a few official weather observations, just in time. Several hours later, the dull ache behind my kneecaps finally disappeared.

It must be convenient to be a human barometer, able to predict weather with one's knees. But I think I'll stick with ordinary thermometers and barographs. They're cheaper and easier to replace when they break.

The mountain is the same, but the dress code sure has changed. People have been hiking in the White Mountains since the 1800s, when the Appalachian Mountain Club was established. Sensible, practical clothing and gear followed a few decades later.

A Day in the Life

A COLD FRONT BLASTED through Helena, Montana, on December 14, 1924, dropping the temperature from 63°F to -25°F in only 34 hours. That's a temperature swing of 88 degrees. In Fairfield, Montana, a glance at the history books shows the mercury plummeting from 63° to -21° in only 12 hours on the same day. That's the power of an invisible, moving wall of chilled air brutally shoving warmer air out of its way.

Cold fronts and violent shifts in the weather have occurred for millennia, but only in the last few centuries have humans been able to quantify those changes with instruments and gauges. Only in the last one hundred years have we truly started to understand what causes them.

The more we know about the atmosphere, the better we get at predicting its moods. The more data we feed into meteorological supercomputers, the better our long-range forecasts become.

Weather satellites, radiosondes, and thousands of reporting stations around the globe provide us with more data than ever before. A few clicks at the keyboard can call up the current temperature in Honolulu, Harrisburg, or Hong Kong. A few seconds is all it takes to learn that the Earth's average temperature is 59 degrees Fahrenheit, that thermometers in Libya peaked at 58°C (136°F) in 1922, and that on March 21, 1983, a tornado funnel unexpectedly dropped thousands of seashells on Stoke-in-Kent, England.

Weather aficionados keep track of dates, temperatures, peak gusts, and other statistics the way baseball fans remember batting averages and RBIs. Consider that in just four paragraphs, I've already listed nine numbers and three dates.

Here's another: On July 4, 1776, Declaration of Independence author Thomas Jefferson took the time to note that the temperature in Philadelphia was exactly 72.5°.

Jefferson was the eighteenth century equivalent of a weather nerd. He hoped to establish a nationwide network of weather observers, but left office years later with his dream unfulfilled.

Fortunately another American, James Tilton, had the same idea. Tilton was the U.S. Army's Surgeon General. In 1814, during the war of 1812, he officially started the first nationwide weather service. Tilton ordered doctors under his command to keep track of the weather on a daily basis.

No one paid him much attention. By 1840, there still were only a few dozen army camps monitoring the weather with poorly calibrated instruments and spotty records. Apparently it was easy to ignore the boss when he couldn't check up on employees by telephone—or even by telegraph.

The invention of the telegraph in the mid-1800s sparked a revolution in weather observation and forecasting, and made Tilton's and Jefferson's vision a reality. For the first time, it was possible to receive up-to-date weather reports from cities hundreds of miles apart. That allowed the creation of the first weather maps and the first reliable forecasts, or "probabilities" as they were called prior to 1876. "Probabilities" were renamed "indications" between December 1876 and April 1, 1889, when the word "forecasts" appeared in the lexicon for the first time.

Suddenly, weather observation had a practical, immediate purpose.

The telegraph allowed Joseph Henry of the Smithsonian Institute to create a network of 150 weather outposts in 1849. In 1870, Congress established the U.S. Army Signal Corps, a precursor to what later became the U.S. Weather Bureau and today's National Weather Service.

Researchers launch a weather balloon from the summit.

"THE BEST WEATHER INSTRUMENT yet devised is a pair of human eyes," meteorologist Harold Gibson told *The New York Times* in 1984. "Looking out the window is the most important thing if you want to know what's going on."

In the nineteenth and twentieth centuries, thousands of weather observers across the country did just that. They lived lives and followed routines as depicted in the book *Isaac's Storm*. They used their eyes, their intuition, and their experience to augment data provided by thermometers and barometers.

In the twenty-first century, the days of manned weather

outposts are largely over. Satellites, automated sensors, and other technology are rapidly taking the place human weather observers. At small airports, ASOS instrumentation has replaced the human eye. Although thousands of people, called cooperative weather observers, still file daily weather reports with the National Weather Service, and the human touch is still present in forecasting offices, the era of large, official, manned observing outposts is over.

One of the last few human-run weather observatories in the world exists in New Hampshire atop 6,288-foot-high Mount Washington. There, the basic routine today is much like it was fifty years or even a hundred years ago—though even on Mount Washington, the times they are a-changing.

A U.S. Army Signal Corps station existed on Mount Washington in the 1880s. In 1932, that station was replaced by a privately run, civilian weather outpost called the Mount Washington Observatory. Employees at the observatory continue to monitor and record the weather today.

Living and working atop a stormy mountain isn't your typical job. Five o'clock rush hour isn't a problem, but blinding, blowing snow and 20-foot snowdrifts sometimes are. Interrupting work to care for a frostbitten hiker is another occasional novelty of employment on Mount Washington.

Early one January, the temperature dipped below zero Fahrenheit. Snow and fog swirled in the sky, and the instruments recorded gusts above 90 mph. One of our interns from Plymouth State College had just gone outside to collect the precipitation can—a large, cylindrical object that's difficult to hold on to in strong winds. Coming back inside, covered in snow and rime, she exclaimed, "It was so windy, it was like trying to wrestle with a five-hundred-pound pig!" That's not the sort of comment you'd hear around the water cooler at an office in Boston.

WHY WOULD ANYONE WANT to live and work in a place where hurricane-force winds howl a hundred days a year?

The appeal of working on a mountaintop isn't so much the extremes. It's the variety. Once there was an undercast, a rippling sea of clouds with the mountaintop poking up in the middle like a lonely island. I kept wishing I had a canoe; I wanted to paddle across the mile-high "waves." Blue sky arced overhead, while below, the sea of clouds extended 90 miles in every direction. It lasted like that for three days.

Of course, that meant that down in the valley people suffered under a dark, dreary gray overcast. I remember meeting a pair of hikers. "We saw the picture on your web page and had to climb up," they said. "We haven't seen the sun for a week!"

What's a typical day like on the summit? Well, there's really no such thing as "typical" on Mount Washington. Each season serves up a different set of demands and responsibilities, and each new day of the week requires a slightly different routine. On any given day, an observer is required to be many things: meteorologist, computer worker, tour guide, janitor, repairman, accountant, researcher, clerk, proofreader, chef, radio personality, teacher, medic, volunteer coordinator, and more. It's a "many hats" job. Due to the elevation, we also like to joke that it's "the highest paying job in New England."

Despite that disclaimer, I'm going to summarize as best as possible a day on the job at the top of Mount Washington. The following is a nuts-and-bolts account of an actual summit workday at the start of the new millennium. (Some details have since changed, and continue to change as new technologies enter the scene. This is truly a last glimpse of a dying era.)

Imagine yourself working on the summit on a winter day. The schedule is hectic, but you're guaranteed to have an ice time. (No pun unintended.) It's Tuesday, the day before the weekly shift change. This is the story of a typical workday at one of the world's last manned weather outposts.

4:00 A.M.

Wake up. Your first responsibility of the day is to feed the cat. (Don't worry, Nin will remind you—loudly—if you forget.) Fix coffee if you are so inclined. The first few hours of the morning are often the busiest, due to the time pressure of forecast preparation and radio shows, so you head upstairs immediately. (Get dressed first, though.) Breakfast will wait until the radio shows are done.

Thar's cold in them thar hills! A weather observer checks the temperature on a chilly morning.

4:15 to 5:00 A.M.

The summit is in the fog, 17 degrees, with winds at 110 mph, so rime ice is accumulating rapidly on the instruments. Time to de-ice. (You can tell because the Hays wind chart is reading abnormally low.) After you put on wind pants, a coat, gloves, hat, balaclava, facemask, and goggles, you look like you're dressed for a trip to the moon; you're now protected from frostbite. Climb up the tower stairs and ladders, past the Cold Room, to the exposed parapet, where many of the instruments are kept. Fight against the wind, climb to the very top, and de-ice. It's a good way to get some exercise, too. Then return inside and shed a few layers of clothes.

Rime is basically "frozen cloud."

Now it's time to get busy with the daily forecast sheet. Using the Internet, take a look at the latest Weather Channel weather map, satellite images, and Doppler radar. Print out the coded regional weather summary and "plain language" weather summary from the National Weather Service. Also look at and print out the zone forecasts for New Hampshire, extended outlooks, the recreation forecast, and state summary. Sometimes you may also want to print out the latest coded METAR reports from all stations in the state.

Using these documents and maps as references, prepare the daily forecast. (It's a single page we fax to the valley office and other locations every morning.) You can call up the template in Microsoft Word. Update all the highs, lows, winds, and expected weather conditions for Tuesday through Saturday. At the top, note any special NWS watches or warnings (e.g. flood warnings, high wind warnings). You must also update the almanac (records for the calendar day), as well as sunrise and sunset times. Refer to yesterday's summary to list the weather events of the past 24 hours.

Wind direction always refers to the direction the wind is blowing from, not the direction it's blowing to. So a northwest wind blows from the northwest toward the southeast.

4:50 A.M.

It's time to take your first observation, which means putting all those clothes on again and going back outside. This is an *hourly* observation, as opposed to a *synoptic*, so it will only take a minute or two. On your way outside, check the instruments for icing. In conditions like these, chances are you will need to climb up the tower to de-ice once again. Then finish and code the observation and send it via modem to the National Weather Service in Bismarck, North Dakota.

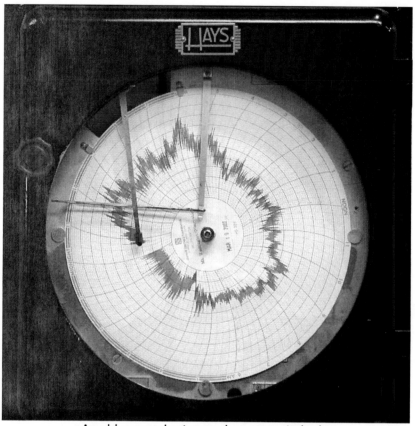

An old paper chart records a very windy day.

Now you can finish the daily weather page. There's a section for "current summit conditions." Use the data from the latest observation. Save the document and print out a copy. Proofread carefully. Go into the radio room and, using a program on the Research_3 computer, fax the daily weather page to the ten to fifteen locations that have requested it. (The list varies but usually includes the valley office, Mount Washington Auto Road office, Cog Railway, Appalachian Mountain Club, Eastern Mountain

Sports, and others.)

At the photocopier, make several copies of the daily weather report. You need to post them at these locations: the weather desk, by the downstairs phone in the living quarters, and on the weather display board. (In the summer, copies are also posted at the Mount Washington State Park ranger's desk and museum.)

5:00 A.M.

The first radio show is coming up at 5:30, so you need to prepare a script. Look over the maps and forecasts again. This is a short, taped show for New Hampshire Public Radio. You need to sound professional.

Start by writing a few words about the weather map: "High pressure is building into New England, but a low over the Great Lakes will…" Then briefly list the highs, lows, and outlook for the south, central, seacoast, and northern parts of the state. Mention the expected conditions for tonight across the state, and conclude with a forecast for the summit. Try to make it lively, interesting, and unique. (For example, "This is the 48th day this year with winds above hurricane force!")

Perhaps you'll say, "A frontal system and a warm air mass will bring New England a mix of rain, sleet, and snow later this weekend…"

Air masses are large sections of air that have a fairly consistent temperature and humidity. As they move, the temperature and moisture content of the land and water they pass over will affect them. Also, the sun will be rising or setting, adding or removing heat from the equation. Gradually, the characteristics of an air mass change.

For example, a cold air mass plunging south from Canada will encounter more and more heat. Eventually it will cease to have the characteristics it started with.

Air masses form when a large area is exposed to similar conditions—similar amounts of sunshine and heat, for example. Meanwhile, a distant area will be exposed to different amounts of heat or moisture. Where the two air masses meet, there will be a front and some interesting, perhaps violent, weather.

Once, during a 5:30 radio forecast, an observer named Nate stumbled over the words "air mass." He finished his report and came downstairs, where the rest of the crew was eating breakfast. He was embarrassed, his face red. "I learned something today," he announced. "Never use the words warm and mass unless they are separated by the word air." Apparently Nate had just told tens of thousands of listeners that a warm mass was moving into New England.

So be careful what you say. Read your script to yourself a few times, making sure the wording sounds right. Make the necessary adjustments.

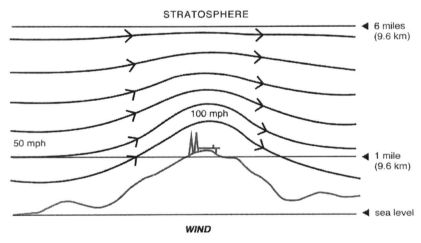

STRATOSPHERE

◀ 6 miles (9.6 km)

100 mph

50 mph

◀ 1 mile (9.6 km)

◀ sea level

WIND

Most clouds, storms, and water vapor exist in the troposphere, the lowest layer of the atmosphere. Stick a mountain in the way of a storm system, and the result is similar to sticking your thumb halfway over the end of a garden hose—the wind (and water) will go faster.

5:15 A.M.

Usually, this is when the phone rings for the first time. No one else is awake yet, so you answer. This is what you hear: "Hello, I'm thinking of hiking up today. Do you think this wind is going to calm down later? Would tomorrow be a better day? What's the weekend look like?" Politely answer the questions, but try to keep the call short, because it's a busy part of the day. If you still have a few minutes before the New Hampshire Public Radio show, start to check and correct yesterday's weather summary (METAR, synoptic, F-6, and station pressure paperwork).

5:30-5:35 A.M.

NHPR calls. Count down "3...2...1" and then tape your weather report. Keep it no longer than 45 seconds, because it's used at the top of the hour during *Morning Edition*. If you run long or mess up (you never do, of course) you'll have to re-tape it.

5:35-6:15 A.M.

The daily forecast pages on the observatory's web page must also be updated. Click the icon on the Observer_1 computer, enter the password, and type away. Unlike the daily weather fax, you must now write a paragraph or two about the weather map, in addition to weather forecasts for the summit and valley (today, tonight, and tomorrow), almanac data, current conditions, and total snowfall for the month. Once you're finished, exit the template, call up the web page and check for typos. Correct if necessary.

Around this time, a fax arrives from the Appalachian Mountain Club, listing the valley weather conditions, snowstake reading, and statistics for the previous 24 hours. You will use this information for several upcoming radio shows, so make a note of the data, then file the form. Later, you will use this information yet again as part of an ongoing snowstake study by Blue Hill Observatory.

At 5:45, the instruments need to be de-iced again, so you climb up to the tower. On the way down, you notice ice enclosing the thermoshack, which turns it into an icebox and makes the temperature seem lower than it truly is. This means you must de-ice the vents on the shack to allow some airflow. As long as you're already bundled up and outside, take the weather observation. Go back inside, continue with the indoor readings (windspeed, barograph, *etc.*), code it, and send it to the National Weather Service. That brings you right up to six o'clock.

6:00-7:00 A.M.

The phone rings again—another hiker. After you hang up, you decide it's a good time to do the "daily walkaround." In the winter, no State Park rangers are present, and the observatory crew serves as caretaker for the building. So grab a pen, a clipboard, and a checklist and "check" the entire building, upstairs and down. Look for any broken windows, snowdrifts inside (we really do get them) or other problems. Several power meters must be read and reported so that we can keep a record of electricity consumption. A bottle of antifreeze is kept by the front door; pick it up and shake it, make sure it hasn't frozen— it's a test for antifreeze in the pipes. Go back into the furnace room and record the daily fuel consumption, condition of the two furnaces, level of fresh water and gray water in the holding tanks, and the sewage. If everything's okay, you're done with the walkaround. If there's a problem, you need to fix it. (You may have to wait until the radio shows are over.)

At 6:30, it's time to collect the precipitation can, which involves a 300-foot walk across the summit cone. Doesn't sound too far, but with 110 mph gusts, it's hard to stay on your feet—and with thick fog, it's sometimes hard enough just to *see* your feet! (That's why we sometimes send interns instead.) Bundle up into the usual outdoor gear, tuck the replacement "precip" can under your arm, and walk to the front door. Here, you may need to stop and put crampons on your feet, to provide traction on the ice. Then you struggle through the gusts to the precip can, switch them quickly (don't lose your grip, or the wind will blow the can to North Conway), and carry the "used" can back indoors. Take off your crampons, but don't shed all the other layers just yet—you need to go back outside again in a few minutes.

Back in the weather room, first measure the unmelted snow in the precip can to the nearest 0.1 inch (this will be converted to millimeters when you report it officially). Go to the darkroom sink, pour some very hot water into a container, and measure it. Then take that hot water and pour it into the precip can (so it melts the snow and ice). Next, measure the liquid water to the nearest 0.01 inch. Subtract the amount of hot water you added, and record the liquid water content. Make a note of the data on a scrap of paper.

On February 9, 2003, a fire destroyed two generator buildings on the summit, including the old TV-8 transmitter building. The fire knocked out communications, put radio stations off the air, and prompted an evacuation of the observatory, which was left without heat or electricity.

The abrupt change to the summit infrastructure forced a change in the daily routine. The Cog Railway transported two (smaller) generators to the summit three months later. As of this writing, a state park ranger is on hand in the winter to oversee the generators and building maintenance. Long-term plans to provide power to the summit will bring more changes to both the infrastructure and the routine in the years ahead.

Sawdust from the Log

"When I went to get the precipitation can tonight, I found the fox outside. He was feasting on the moths that were flocking in droves to the walkway lights. As they landed on the ground, he would quickly lap them up. He didn't pay much heed to me."

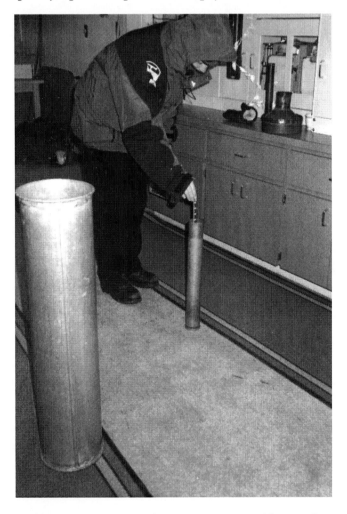

Every six hours a crew member must go outside to change the precipitation can. Hold on tight, or the wind will rip the can out of your hands and hurl it down to North Conway.

6:35-6:55 A.M.

Every three hours, you must log onto the helipad computer in order to check the ASOS anemometers. If everything is working properly, note it on the checklist and log off. If one or more anemometers aren't working, make a note of the problem, describe the current weather conditions, and call the appropriate person. It may be necessary for you to walk down to the helipad (about 1/4th of a mile). But first...

...it's time to complete the first "synoptic" observation of the day. Head back upstairs, de-ice the instruments, and check the current weather conditions. Indoors, you must check the atmospheric pressure, average windspeed, peak gust in the past 10 minutes, and all other relevant data. When you are finished, you will have two reports. The METAR report is the simpler one. Here's an example:

KMWN 131148Z 27077G91KT 220V320 0SM +SHSN FZFG M08/M08 RMK PK WND 28099/31 PRESRR SHSNB05 LGT ICG SUN DMLY VSBL

Sawdust from the Log

May 6. "Wet cat footprints all over the METAR sheet, minimum temp of 40 degrees, and only a tiny patch of snow remains on the deck."

The code packs of lot of information into just one or two lines. Translated into everyday English, here's what it says: "Hi, this is Mount Washington calling at 11:48 Greenwich Mean Time on the 13th day of the month." So far we've only covered KMWN and 131148Z. Here's the rest: "Winds are variable from the southwest to northwest, but mostly west at about 270 degrees. They're averaging 77 knots and gusting to 91 knots. Visibility is less than 330 feet. We have snow flurries, plus freezing fog, lightly depositing rime ice. Temperature and dew point are both –8° Celsius. The peak wind in the past hour occurred at 31 minutes past the hour; it came from the west at 99 knots. Barometric pressure is rising rapidly. Oh yes, remember those snow flurries? Well, they started at five past the hour. The sun is dimly visible through the fog."

The "synoptic" code goes into more detail and for that reason takes a little longer. Again, an example:

70263 11/00 92777 11078 21078 38022 53099 60241 77374
333 11064 21086 4/010 70638 90937 93108 938// LOXDA

Sometimes less really is more. Those two, short lines contain all the information of a typical METAR report, plus addition detailed data about atmospheric pressure, cloud types, precipitation amounts, and tied and broken records. The third group of numbers alone, 92777, informs you that the sky is obscured, wind is from the west at a direction of 270 degrees, averaging 77 knots.

Here's a complete rundown of what those clumps of numbers tell you, in order. Feel free to skip ahead, or maybe take a few aspirin.

["Hello there, National Weather Service! Mount Washington here."; has there been any precipitation in the past six hours? (yes), have there been obstructions to vision (yes), the sky is currently obscured, visibility is less than 330 feet, wind direction is from the west (270 degrees) averaging 77 knots, the current temperature is -7.8° Celsius, the dew point is the same, the current pressure is 802.2 millibars, the pressure was formerly falling, but is now rising rapidly, the pressure has risen by 9.9 millibars in the past three hours, 24 millimeters of precipitation have fallen in the past six hours, it is snowing heavily, and we have had snow and fog during the past six hours. The maximum temperature recorded in that time was -6.4° Celsius, the minimum was -8.6 degrees, an average of 10 centimeters of snow covers the station, and a total of 63.8 mm of precipitation has fallen in the past 24 hours. Precipitation began more than three hours ago; there have been two or more periods of precipitation lasting between six and twelve hours, and 10.8 cm of snow (unmelted) have fallen in the past six hours. We have also experienced glaze icing (freezing rain) during the past six hours, and set a new record low temperature for the day.]

Without going into any more detail (I can hear sighs of relief) you must also fill out the appropriate columns on the B-16 form at this time. That only takes a minute. But hurry, because coming up right away is...

7:00 A.M.

...the next radio show, the Appalachian Mountain Club huts report. Over the radio, say "This is unit 20 standing by with the weather." When signaled, give all the same information you will later give to WMOU and WMWV—only read it very slowly, because the AMC hut crews are writing it all down by hand. They will post it for the public. If the phone rings in the middle of this report (it often does), politely explain that you are on the air and ask the caller to call back in half an hour. When the AMC report is done, sign off and...

...immediately after you finish, you are paged on the intercom. This week's volunteer cooks are awake now, making breakfast for a crew of researchers who are staying on the summit. (On other days of the week, it could be EduTrips, hiking trip guests, or visiting media.) The volunteers tell you they're not sure exactly how formal a breakfast to prepare. They also have questions about a group of college students and researchers coming up later in the day. They're good volunteers, but not used to cooking for so many. You go downstairs and spend a few moments showing them how to operate the food processor, and also where to find certain food items in the pantry. You also write up a "to-do" list for them, listing how many people to prepare for at breakfast, lunch, and dinner.

7:10-7:33 A.M.

Use the next few minutes to finish correcting yesterday's weather summary. (You will have been working on it all morning long, during "spare" moments.) This activity involves proofing all columns, codes, and calculations on the following forms: METAR, B-16, B-15, F-6, and station pressure sheet. Make red pencil corrections as necessary.

You are currently training the new night observer, so make a list of any recurring errors, "misses," and other items on the official forms, plus explanations as to why these items needed correction. Plan to go over with them with the new observer later in the day.

The next radio show is coming up, so begin to prepare your notes. This is a longer, live show—about three to five minutes— broadcast throughout Coos County, New Hampshire, on WMOU and WXLQ.

7:33-7:40 A.M.

After some on-air banter with the radio announcer, he introduces you, and you start your radio weather report. Begin with current summit conditions (temperature, max and min temperatures, average windspeed and peak gust, pressure, precipitation, visibility, etc). Next, provide the current conditions at Pinkham Notch. Then spend a minute or two talking about the weather map and what it means for the North Country over the next few days. Close with the valley forecast for today, tonight, and tomorrow, followed by the summit forecast, and finally the extended outlook for the region.

7:41 to 7:50 A.M.

The next radio show is coming up in just a few minutes, but first you need to take another observation. Bundle up in the usual apparel, run upstairs and outside. De-ice if necessary. Back inside, code the report and send it to the National Weather Service, then get ready for the next radio show.

7:50 to 7:55 A.M.

Now it's time for WMWV. It's a three-minute show, transmitted in Carroll County and western Maine. It's a bit shorter than the previous show, but in addition to a weather summary, you must also include the latest avalanche bulletin, ski conditions on the Sherburne Ski Trail, and other information for outdoor enthusiasts.

7:55 to 8:25 A.M. (various tasks)

Whew! The radio shows are coming fast and furious now. If you haven't finished the hourly observation yet, do so now. Another show is coming up right away.

After WMWV, immediately begin the WHOM radio report. They will call you. This is a short, taped, 30-second report, so write out a script first. It's heard by many, from Portland to Brattleboro to Nashua.

Resort Sports Network, a local cable TV channel, will call next. Go over all the weather information and hiker/skier information one more time. You usually know it all by heart now. This show features more chitchat and improvisation than most of the others, and you will often be asked trivia about the summit, historical information, personal experiences, and so forth. Trivia can include the fact that Mount Washington's maximum yearly snowfall was 566.4 inches in the winter of 1968-69, which is impressive but can't compare with the whopping 1,224.5 inches that buried Mount Rainier in 1971-72. When it comes to extremes, Mount Washington can boast 300 days per year with fog and more than a hundred days a year with winds above hurricane force.

In 1857, a Dutch meteorologist named Buys Ballot discovered what we now know as Buys Ballot's Law: In the Northern Hemisphere, if you stand outside with the wind at your back, high pressure is on your right and low pressure is on your left.

With a name like Buys Ballot, it's a good thing he chose a career as a scientist, rather than as a politician.

8:30 to 9:00 A.M.

Congratulations! You've finished what is often the most hectic part of the day. Take a deep breath...and then get busy again. (First, if your stomach's grumbling and the phone is not yet ringing off the hook, you might manage to sneak downstairs for a quick breakfast.)

At this time of day, it's necessary to change the NECI air filter. (Various research experiments change from year to year and season to season, but NECI is one good example.) You must get dressed in a Tyvek suit, hood, facemask, and plastic gloves to avoid contaminating the filter. In the Cold Room of the tower, note the time and current reading, then switch off the equipment. Pull the old filter inside and extract it (you may need to chip some ice first, before pulling it in through the window). Place the old filter in a sealed bag, label it, and store it in the freezer. Replace it with a new filter. (It will be switched again tomorrow). Reset the counter to zero and note the time. The supply of filters is low, so you need to remember to email UNH—the University of New Hampshire—later today to let them know. For now, get out of the Tyvek suit and head back downstairs to the weather room.

The phone rings a few more times in the next half hour: hikers, observatory members, perhaps a reporter asking about snowfall or yesterday's search-and-rescue operation. At 8:50 or 8:55, it's time to take and report another hourly METAR observation. (Nin sometimes helps with the paperwork.)

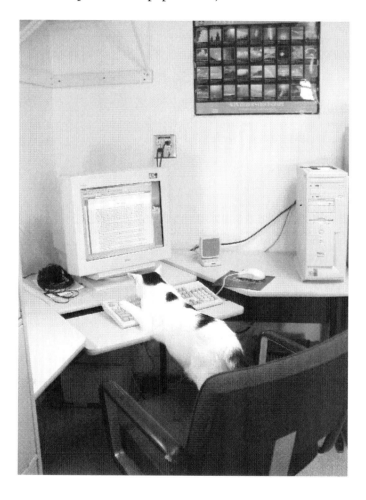

9:00 A.M.

A few of the overnight guests wander upstairs and chat with you. One of the researchers asks if you can spare a few moments later to show him where certain records are kept and what the codes mean. You glance up at the clock and promise to do so after 10 A.M. It's just too busy right now, you explain apologetically. A visiting reporter also requests an interview with you later in the day.

There are several tasks that urgently need to be done today, so you write up a "to do" list for the entire crew. Some of these tasks you can delegate, others you do yourself. What are these tasks? Shoveling snow under the A-frame and by the front door. Chipping ice in the tower parapet and cold room floor. Fixing the broken door handle. Sealing and caulking the lower and side doors for the winter. And so much more.

Tuesday is the day before shift change, so you must now prepare a fresh food/dairy order for Guy Gosselin (he'll bring it to the base tomorrow). First, you must check the schedule for the upcoming week—how many EduTrips, special trips, researchers, volunteers, and crew members will be present? How many meals will need to be served during the next eight days? The number could be as low as five people per day, or as many as twenty. You don't want to under-order, because the mountain environment does not permit any quick trips to the grocery store if you run out of anything. You don't want to over-order, either, because of the cost. So you carefully check the two refrigerators, three freezers, and pantry for leftovers. Since paper towels are running low, you place an order for those as well. (About five or six boxes of food will arrive tomorrow and need to be put away, rotating the stock so that older items are in front and get used first.) At this time, you also prepare a preliminary "request" list for your shift's next week on the summit.

9:30 A.M.

The weather is easing up a bit, with intermittent fog. You change the "comment" line on the data logger to reflect this fact. Visitors to the observatory's web page—as well as the Auto Road staff in summer—can check this to view the current summit conditions. This is a task that will be done periodically throughout the day.

9:45 A.M.

Again, log onto the helipad computers and verify that all ASOS anemometers are functioning. Fill out the checklist.

Next, it is time to do another synoptic observation. While you're outside, de-ice if needed. Code and transmit the observation to the NWS. Bombardier operator Chris Uggerholt also calls on the radio at this time. He is bringing up some equipment, students, and researchers and needs to know the current conditions. "It's getting better," you tell him, "But visibility is still only a hundred feet." Chris tells you he'll call for an update when he reaches Cragway, a point halfway up the mountain.

Sawdust from the Log

February 2. "The snow tractor is forced to turn back after a four-hour battle with a crusty road."

9:50-10:00 A.M.

After the 0950 observation, it's time to do the twice-daily COSMO check. This is a long-term research experiment for the University of New Hampshire. Fill out the appropriate forms, do the calculations, and initial the appropriate columns.

You have now completed the first six hours of the day. The

next six to ten hours will be similar, minus the radio shows. Every hour, you will make a short weather observation. Every three hours you will do a longer "synoptic" observation, and will also check the status of the ASOS anemometers. You will be the observer on call to answer phones, play host to the media, coordinate and introduce arriving researchers, and handle emergencies. (If you have an intern or observer-in-training, you can try to delegate the phone-answering duties—but you will discover that it's usually for you anyway.) Continuously, you will de-ice.

WHEN I FIRST TYPED up a draft of "A Day in the Life of a Weather Observer" and showed it to some coworkers, they said, "We feel exhausted just reading all that." Just think how tired they felt *doing* all that.

Time to pick up the pace. In order to keep the rest of this chapter short (well, shorter), I'll just list some of the additional duties that might fill the late morning/early afternoon hours:

Marty Engstrom calls from TV-8, saying he caught two desperate hikers trying to break into the Yankee building for shelter. He's sending them over your way. "They look like they're in trooubllllle," he drawls in his distinctive accent. You meet the hikers at the front door and assess the situation. The rules say no one can come in, but you don't want to cause anyone's death. It turns out they're adequately dressed but slightly hypothermic. You let them into the alcove and bring them hot chocolate, let them warm up for a while. After checking the weather updates, you advise them to head down the Auto Road, which is longer but easier than Tuckerman Ravine. You give them directions to take the Auto Road to the Old Jackson Road Trail back to Pinkham.

Marty Engstrom, famous in Maine and northern Hampshire

for his bow tie, trademark smile, and nightly weather reports, worked as an engineer at WMTW TV-8's summit transmitter building for more than three decades. The WMTW crew were the observatory's nearest (and only) neighbors. Sometimes we'd brave the winds and walk across the summit cone to go trick-or-treating, or share a Thanksgiving dinner. ("Marty on the Mountain" retired in 2002.)

The FAA and the U.S. Army have used Mount Washington as a testing ground, taking advantage of the peak's steady supply of ice and fog.

Later, you check the emergency hiker register by the front door. Bring additional forms, in case they've all been used. Replace the pencil if it's missing, test the intercom.

Mike Pelchat, State Park Manager, calls from Cannon Mountain. He's concerned about reports of a warm front and heavy, cold rain due in the next few days. He asks you (or Chris) to check the building's heat tapes.

If major melting starts to occur, combined with heavy rain, you may need to set up a sump pump and hose in order to keep the bottom of the tower from flooding into the living quarters. The necessary equipment is kept in the shop.

The previous day's B-16 form must be inked, checked, and filed. You may delegate the inking to an intern or junior staff member, before verifying, checking, and filing the final form.

CRREL multicylinders, another ongoing research experiment. The initials CRREL stand for Cold Regions Research and Engineering Laboratory, a research branch of the U.S. Army. The goal is for each observer to do two multicylinder runs per day, if weather conditions permit. The experiment involves taking a stopwatch and clipboard, exiting the upper tower door, and hooking up the instrument to a motor, and exposing the cylinders for 5 to 20 minutes (depending on the type of icing—light, moderate, or heavy). Record the current weather conditions and temperatures while the multicylinder is collecting ice. After an adequate amount of ice has been collected, retrieve the cylinders, note the "stop" time, and bring it all down into the Cold Room. With a caliper, measure the width of each of the five cylinders, plus weight and length, as well as type of ice. Note any special occurrences. Downstairs, type the data into the CRREL program, print out the graph, fill out the appropriate checklist.

The Forest Service calls, asking for all weather data between 4 P.M. and 10 P.M. on such-and-such a day. A search-and-rescue was in progress at that time, you remember. "It's for a lawsuit," the Forest Service tells you. You email them the requested data.

A member calls. "I was married on the summit on July 4, 1982, and I remember it being really windy. Always wondered, just how windy was it?" You check the records and tell them.

A visiting researcher asks some questions about data being used for his experiment. He asks you to give him a primer in METAR so that he can understand some of the codes.

SOPs (an acronym for "Standard Operating Procedure") need to updated: morning shift, evening shift, furnace operation, etc.

Fresh water is low, so you must pump. The pump is located in the far end of the building, in an unheated section. You check/change the filters in the tank room, close the three valves along the corridor, and insert the fuses which power the pump. First, drain the water through a hose out the front door until it runs clear (it often comes out of the well very murky at the start.) When it's clear, raise the switch, which sends it to Tank #1 at the other end of the building. (Be careful—if you have forgotten or missed a valve here or there, a waterfall will start to cascade down the corridor.) Make a note to remind yourself that water is pumping, then go on to other tasks; it will take about 40 minutes to fill the tank. When done, open all drain valves and put away the hose.

Fuel is also low. Call Marty at TV-8, verify how much fuel is needed (you don't want to request too much and overfill the tanks) and open the valve. Note on the walkaround checklist how much fuel was pumped, and when.

Peter Crane faxes a list of items he would like removed from the summit museum and shipped to the valley museum with the next down-going trip. Books, posters, postcards of Nin, etc. You grab a coat and flashlight (the museum is in the unheated part of the building), locate the items, fill out an inventory form, and put it all in a bag to go to the valley.

CBS Studios in New York calls, asking to speak to the observer-on-duty. They're doing a feature on Hurricane Mitch and the power of weather, and would like to speak to someone about "what it's like to be out in hurricane winds. We figured you guys would know." They ask to tape the interview, which lasts 20 minutes; only 30 seconds or so are used in the final show.

The call from CBS reminds you—your inbox contains several

messages from other TV stations, including CNN, a second station in White River Junction, Vermont, and a third from Portland, Maine. They have all requested overnight visits. Each station intends to do a feature story about the observatory, which is good publicity. Your job is to schedule them (obviously not at the same time), making sure there is enough bunk space and room on the snow tractor. Media visits cannot conflict with EduTrips or visits by large numbers of researchers or student trips. First, you look over the schedule. Check by phone with various observatory departments to see if they have any special trips planned. Verify Chris Uggerholt's schedule and vacation time (CNN can't make it to the summit if there's no one available to drive the SnoCat.) Then call back each station with the open dates. Caution them that these days are likely to fill up quickly. First come, first served. After the dates for visits have been set, mail out media guides, describing weather conditions, safety measures, what to expect, and what guests should bring in terms of clothing and gear.

E-mailed questions from the web page also must be answered. Some examples:

"What causes a rainbow?"

"Please send me more information about EduTrips."

"I heard a typhoon broke your record. Is that true?"

"Why is the web camera always gray?"

Sawdust from the Log

"Not fully prepared, physically or gear-wise, for the arduous journey to the summit in full winter conditions, the hikers were cold and wet and stranded on the summit as the fog rolled back in. Turn back before the daylight runs out on you! Head down away from the bad weather, not into it!"

Some meteorologists hoof it to the summit, even in winter, but it's easier to get to the Wednesday morning staff meeting on time if you ride in the snow tractor. A typical winter commute up the Mount Washington Auto Road takes about two hours. Blowing snow and zero visibility can increase that to six hours or even cancel the trip altogether.

Don't forget to fill out your timesheet. Take care of interoffice correspondence.

Every month, you must record the Shaw readings. Bundle up in the unusual outdoor attire, grab a clipboard and keys, and walk out to the original observatory building on the other side of the summit cone. Sometimes the outer lock freezes, so you may need to take a heat gun and warm the lock to get inside. Next, head up the stairs, unlock the upper door, and record the readings on ten different power meters. Also note and record the indoor temperature. (It's kept at about 40 degrees Fahrenheit, above freezing.) Downstairs, make sure the furnace is working properly. Note any damage to the building (either from weather—the floor usually turns into an ice rink—or from trespassers. Desperate hikers sometimes break into this building in search of shelter). Make a copy of the meter readings, file them, and mail the originals to Shaw Communications.

Before tomorrow morning, you must prepare, print out, and make copies of an agenda for the next staff meeting. Include the minutes from the previous meeting, and email to the Executive Director and President of the Board of Trustees when done.

If there is a heavy snowfall, high winds, or severe icing, several TV meteorologists are likely to call you to ask a few questions, to add some interest to their shows.

Another phone call, this time from the volunteers who are scheduled to work on the summit in two weeks time. Due to a family emergency, they have to cancel. They apologize. You must now find a replacement volunteer on short notice. Otherwise, the summit crew will need to cook and wash dishes for EduTrips and all other guests. (Sometimes that happens and no replacements can be found, so you just have to grin and bear it, in addition to your normal duties.) But you hope to avoid that situation. Looking through the archive of volunteer applications, you start to make phone calls, leaving messages if no one is home. Retirees who have previously volunteered on the summit are your best bet at this point—it will be difficult for most people to take time away from work on only two week's notice. Still, you leave eight to ten messages and hope for the best.

The Discovery Channel—the current media group visiting the summit—requests permission to follow you around with a camera, to illustrate to their viewers what it's like on the summit. You oblige.

The NAWAS "hotline" rings, and you hear a voice over the

speaker: "All New Hampshire stations please acknowledge roll call." NAWAS is the National Warning System, allowing quick communication between various state and federal posts in the event of a weather emergency—or other disaster. (NAWAS's original purpose in the 1950s was to notify of an impending nuclear attack.) You wait for the signal, say "Mount Washington, test," and then note the date and time of the test on the checklist.

Train your interns (if you have any) how to use Microsoft Excel, and then set them up with a data entry project. One ongoing project is the transfer of archived data from B-16s and earlier forms (1935-present) from paper to computer disk, for easier duplication and faster search and retrieval. Many different people and organizations rely on our data, and it's easier to FTP them our historical data rather than photocopying and mailing dozens of old paper forms.

4:30 P.M.

You have now been on duty for more than twelve hours, and technically your day is done. At the very least, you no longer need to do hourly observations and are no longer answering the phone. However, it's clean-up day. So you gather the crew together and try to get everyone to tackle cleanup as a team before dinner. This includes:

Clean, mop, and scrub the two bathrooms, replace towels.

Empty trash in all rooms and offices, upstairs and down. Bag all garbage, bring out front to be taken off the summit.

Wash windows and glass on instruments. Dust offices and furniture.

Clean, separate and bag all recyclables; bring out front to be taken down.

Clean all refrigerators remove any "expired" items.

85

Clean kitchen counters and sinks.

Move kitchen table and chairs, sweep kitchen floor, scrub with scrubber, mop.

Remove rugs, then sweep, scrub, and mop all upstairs floors. Return rugs. Vacuum.

Clean/organize the workshop.

Clean/vacuum state park living quarters, which are used for EduTrips and visiting researchers. Make sure the space heaters are turned off so they don't start a fire.

Clean/vacuum/straighten the living room, the six-bunk room, and all crew bunkrooms.

Clean/vacuum/organize the conference room and all upstairs offices.

Nin inspects the crew's work on clean-up day. When Nin retired from the summit in 2008 (to be closer to the veterinarian) a new cat named Marty took over Nin's supervisory duties.

5:00-6:00 P.M.

After working 13+ hours, you finally can start to slow down. The visiting researchers and media guests still ask you questions when they see you in the living room, and you answer politely enough. But you're too tired for chitchat, so you soon head back upstairs and "hide" in your office. Perhaps you and the crew spare 45 minutes for a game of Scrabble. Otherwise, this is a good time to catch up on office e-mails and correspondence, updating SOPs, inventory/orders, and any other tasks you might not have finished earlier in the day. The weekly cleanup (after all, you may have had more than 50 people using the facilities during the week) also continues.

6:00-7:00 P.M.

The night observer, hit by a sudden 95-mph gust of wind, accidentally breaks a psychrometer. You take out a spare thermometer, a wick, and then put together a new psychrometer. At this time, you also send off an e-mail to Jim Mansfield at the National Weather Service office in Gray, Maine, requesting more thermometers. Your supply is getting low.

While you're at it, you decide to do an inventory of all forms and charts. The observatory receives certain forms free from the NWS; others need to be ordered at cost from the appropriate companies. You request additional B-16 forms from Jim Mansfield, and also place an order for thermograph charts (sending a purchase order to the valley office).

As volunteer coordinator for the summit, you must keep up with the paperwork and correspondence: filing applications and questionnaires, sending clothing lists and information updates, scheduling and confirming dates, acquiring and filing injury release forms, writing thank you letters, answering questions, etc. This is a good time of day to catch up on some of that paperwork; a steady supply of new applications and requests is always arriving.

7:00-8:00 P.M.

Dinner. Tonight, as if often the case in winter, you have guests. So the crew cannot relax entirely. You are all still playing host to a certain extent. (Which means you and your shiftmates can't talk openly about office politics, or how hard your day was, or make jokes about the foolish tourist who annoyed you earlier in the day—because that tourist might be eating at the table with you!) The guests are always fascinated with the observatory and want to ask you all about your experiences. You've been so busy throughout the day that this may be their first chance to talk with you. As always, you oblige.

A late-night phone call or two from the valley, and from researchers, usually occurs at dinner. People are either checking on the forecast for tomorrow's weather conditions, coordinating transport, or confirming bunk space. The new volunteers, scheduled to arrive tomorrow, may also call you with last minute questions.

8:00-9:00 P.M.

The volunteers start to wash dishes and take care of final clean-up items. You and the crew head upstairs, briefly, away from the crowds. Now's your chance to talk a little bit, without the constraints of being on-duty and playing host. (On a night without guests, you may even watch a little TV or read a book.)

It's 9 P.M. You're finally done for the day. Time for some well-deserved rest, but don't relax too much. It all starts again in seven hours.

YOU'VE NOW COMPLETED a typical day in the life of a weather observer.

Not every day is the same as this example. In summer, there is less need to de-ice. Instead, you may be giving tours to sightseers or visiting meteorologists. Occasionally (usually after the summer interns leave in August) you may be required to run down to the museum and fill in for the museum attendant for 10 or 15 minutes once or twice a day. Or you may spend half an hour helping to fold t-shirts for the gift shop.

Rather than hypothermic hikers knocking at the front door, Park Manager Mike Pelchat may request the observatory's help searching for and carrying out a hiker with a broken ankle. If that's the case, you are the one who must decide who among the crew is available and capable, and also determine who is going to fill-in for them while they're gone. You must determine whether or not the weather conditions are safe, help pack up the necessary gear (blankets, splints, litter, *etc.*), keep a record of what gear goes out, and make sure it all comes back. (Sometimes it gets mixed in with AVSAR or Appalachian Mountain Club gear and sent down the mountain with the patient.) You may even go yourself—it's been known to happen that a day observer has left for a rescue at 5 P.M., returned at 11:30 P.M., and then started the normal day shift on short sleep at 4 A.M. the next morning.

Certain special responsibilities occur once a month, or periodically throughout the year. On some days, departments in the valley may request your help for special projects. The summit crew was once asked to download surface weather maps and satellite images every three hours over the span of several months, to put into a comparative video loop demonstrating changing weather patterns, for use with educational programs. Summit staff also contribute ideas for museum exhibits. The observer-on-duty often sits in front of a camera, fielding questions about weather from parents and children at the Mount Washington Museum.

The day you've just read about was busier than, say, a typical

Sunday (the easiest part of the workweek) but less busy than some of the extreme workdays that occur in winter, or during holiday weekends in mid-summer. Every day is different.

FROM PEAK TO POLE. Where do people go after living and working at the Home of the World's Worst Weather? More than a dozen Mount Washington Observatory crew members have gone on to work in Antarctica.

Epilogue

I'M A FIRM BELIEVER THAT staff meetings are mostly a waste of time, unless there's free pizza. So when the observatory scheduled an all-staff meeting on the mountaintop on June 8, I brought along a full agenda and an empty stomach.

Just getting everyone assembled in one place at one time took longer than the meeting itself. An unexpected June blizzard turned what should have been a twenty-minute drive into a three-hour transportation nightmare.

Overnight, an inch-and-half of snow had fallen on the peak. Early in the morning, staff members gathered in the Glen House parking lot. We looked up at the summit and saw it smothered in dark gray clouds. Not a good sign. The temperature dropped below freezing, and winds whipped at 60 mph.

The Auto Road staff refused to allow any vehicle above halfway unless it had four-wheel drive and chains on the tires. So much for a quick trip up in the *Weather Notebook* Subaru. The only option left was to shuttle people by truck. Five of the summit staff hitched a ride up in the WMTW-TV 8 truck. The rest waited an hour in hope that the sun would appear and melt some of the snow.

Eventually the lower half of the road was free of ice. That

allowed us to drive to treeline with chainless vehicles. There, we waited. Wind whistled and howled. I put on a hat and gloves and walked a short distance up the road. A few tufts of fog washed by, and clumps of snow decorated the branches of the dwarf spruce.

While we were waiting, the WMTW truck came back down, bringing along with two Observatory crewmembers. They were on their way back down to pick up some pizza; the long commute was making people hungry. We'd left the base shortly after breakfast, and it now appeared that we wouldn't all arrive on the summit until lunch. That's not unusual for winter...but June?

Immediately after dropping off its passengers, the WMTW truck—with one driver and five empty seats—started back up to the summit. "Why don't we get a ride with them, rather than waiting?" someone commented. Everyone agreed—too late. We wistfully watched the nearly empty vehicle pull away and vanish in the fog. So much for that idea.

Eventually, the last eight people (plus seven boxes of pizza) squeezed into a pickup truck for the last trip up. It should be noted that our local pizzeria says it delivers "anywhere in the Gorham area." Alas, that's not true. The summit of Mount Washington is certainly in the Gorham area—we can even see the mill smokestacks in Berlin when the peak isn't in the fog—but they adamantly refuse to deliver. Apparently our driveway's too long.

However, Mr. Pizza was kind enough to bring our lunch to the base of the Auto Road, and that was how eight of us came to be crammed like sardines into the back of the pickup truck, along with boxes of cheese, mushroom, and pepperoni pizza. The weather had warmed a bit, melting some of the snow and ice, but the dirt road still was very soft and muddy. The truck lurched from side to side.

In the back, I heard snippets of conversation: "I'm not sure how much pizza will be left when we get to the top. I'm ready for lunch."

"Ah, that's the advantage of being on the last trip."

In the end, it took a total of five different vehicles, three round-trips from the summit, and nearly three hours to transport the entire observatory crew from the base of the mountain to the peak. By the end of the trip, we were all cold, and so was the pizza.

After an eight-day workweek on the summit, the exhausted crew faces one last chore before they can go home. They must dig out their cars from under a week's worth of snowfall in the parking lot at the foot of the mountain. If the weather is good on shift change day, some of the crew prefer to walk or ski down the Mount Washington Auto Road rather than sit in the back of the slow-moving snow tractor.

Parting Shots

THE VIEW FROM THE OFFICE window (on the rare occasions when the summit is not shrouded in fog) is one of the best perks of the job. A short hike down the trail opens up even more scenic vistas. Enjoy images from the Mount Washington on the following pages.

Visitors to the summit come in all shapes and sizes. This bull moose appears to be hiking up the Appalachian Trail.

A scenic view of the summit of Mount Washington.

I once saw a terrible pun somewhere on the internet: "Many are cold, but few are frozen." I think they were joking about cryogenics, but the pun applies just as well to icy Mount Washington.

Looking for more?

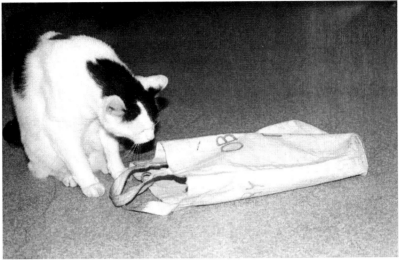

Addition information about the Mount Washington Observatory can be found at www.mountwashington.org. Or write or call:

Mount Washington Observatory
2779 White Mountain Highway
P. O. Box 2310
North Conway NH 03860
(603)-356-2137
info@mountwashington.org

The Mount Washington Observatory advances understanding of the Earth's natural systems by maintaining its mountaintop weather station, conducting research and educational programs, and interpreting the heritage of the Mount Washington region. A dedicated group of more than 100 observers has recorded the world's worst weather since 1932.

Sawdust from the Log
January 3, 2002

"Today we had 98-mph winds! The crew went out to play in it around 9:00 P.M. Exciting! Five hikers in trouble were inside the double Dutch doors for a spot of hot cocoa earlier. Cold and lost in fog, but warmed with hot cocoa, they walked down the Auto Road to Pinkham."

AMONG THE CLOUDS

Acknowledgements

Front cover and interior photographs and illustrations courtesy of the Mount Washington Observatory archives and Mount Washington Museum, except for the following:

Back cover photograph by Anna Porter Johnston

Star trail photograph on page 9 by Brian Post Photography, www.brianpostphoto.com

Illustration on page 26 by Jon Lingel
Images on page 30 and 33 are courtesy of the very useful NOAA Photolibrary: www. photolib.noaa.gov
Photographs on pages 59 and 68 by Eric Pinder
Antarctica photograph on page 90 by Anna Porter Johnston

Chapter Two originally published in *Slate*.

ABOUT THE AUTHOR

Eric Pinder was born in upstate New York, attended college in western Massachusetts, graduated, and some time later drove to northern New Hampshire in a rusty Chevy Nova packed with a few clothes, almost no furniture, and about a dozen boxes of books.

Eric's lifelong interests in science and the outdoors led to jobs at the Appalachian Mountain Club and Mount Washington Observatory. For years he lived and worked as a weather observer atop the snowy, windswept, 6288-foot summit of Mount Washington, the "Home of the World's Worst Weather." His experiences there inspired two books, *Life at the Top* and *Tying Down the Wind*. He also wrote *North to Katahdin*, a book about the appeal of mountains and wilderness.

Eric enjoys hiking and biking up the hills of New Hampshire, but has not yet qualified to join the Four Thousand Footer Club (for people who have climbed each of the state's 48 peaks rising 4000+ feet). He has, however, climbed one of those peaks (Mount Washington) at least 48 times and thinks that ought to count.

He lives in Berlin, New Hampshire.

www.ericpinder.com